Shouting
Won't Grow Dendrites

Other Books by Marcia L. Tate

Worksheets Don't Grow Dendrites: A Multimedia Kit for Professional Development (2006)

Reading and Language Arts Worksheets Don't Grow Dendrites: 20 Literacy Strategies That Engage the Brain (2005)

"Sit and Get" Won't Grow Dendrites: 20 Professional Learning Strategies That Engage the Adult Brain (2004)

Worksheets Don't Grow Dendrites: 20 Instructional Strategies That Engage the Brain (2003)

Marcia L. Tate

Shouting
Won't Grow Dendrites
20
Techniques for Managing a Brain-Compatible Classroom

CORWIN PRESS
A SAGE Publications Company
Thousand Oaks, CA 91320

Illustrations by Robert Greisen.

For information:

 Corwin Press
A Sage Publications Company
2455 Teller Road
Thousand Oaks, California 91320
www.corwinpress.com

Sage Publications Ltd.
1 Oliver's Yard
55 City Road
London EC1Y 1SP
United Kingdom

Sage Publications India Pvt. Ltd.
B-42, Panchsheel Enclave
Post Box 4109
New Delhi 110 017 India

Printed in the United States of America

Library of Congress Cataloging-in-Publication Data

Tate, Marcia L.
Shouting won't grow dendrites: 20 techniques for managing a brain-compatible classroom/Marcia L. Tate.
    p. cm.
Includes bibliographical references and index.
ISBN 978-1-4129-2779-6 (cloth)—ISBN 978-1-4129-2780-2 (pbk.)

 1. Classroom management—United States—Problems, exercises, etc.
2. Teaching—United States—Problems, exercises, etc. I. Title.
LB3013.T366 2007
371.102′4—dc22   2006005413

This book is printed on acid-free paper.

    10   10 9 8 7 6

Acquisitions Editor:	Rachel Livsey
Editorial Assistant:	Phyllis Cappello
Production Editor:	Melanie Birdsall
Typesetter:	C&M Digitals (P) Ltd.
Copy Editor:	Diana Breti
Indexer:	Michael Ferreira
Graphic Designer:	Lisa Miller

Contents

Introduction

During more than 30 years in education, I have learned a great deal about what teachers should and should not do when it comes to managing their classrooms. I have actually seen both of the following scenarios several times:

SCENARIO I ■

Mr. Bledsoe teaches science at Sherman Oaks Middle School. Follow me to his classroom and visualize what a typical day with him would look like.

Students are reluctantly filing into room 310, Mr. Bledsoe's class. They are reluctant because he happens to be one of the most boring, yet sarcastic teachers around. As they enter his room, several students are talking loudly. He immediately shouts at them in an effort to reprimand them for their unruly behavior. They pay him little attention since they have heard him shout so often; they have become accustomed to it. Since the students do not comply with his request for absolute silence, he is now really angry and repeats his request, but louder. They still pay Mr. Bledsoe little attention. You notice that his science classroom consists of lab tables and chairs but is drab and lacks any attention-getting images or hands-on materials in support of the course content.

The bell rings for the start of class, and Mr. Bledsoe instructs students to sit down and open their science textbooks to Chapter 5. He asks them to follow along while he reads part of the chapter aloud. He reads in a monotone, boring fashion so several students begin simultaneous side conversations. Every few paragraphs, he stops and warns students to pay attention because much of what he is reading will be on the pop quiz that he will give when he feels like it or when they need to be taught a lesson about not giving him their undivided attention. The reading aloud goes on for well over 20 minutes.

Mr. Bledsoe then instructs students to get out paper and pencil because he will be lecturing and they will need to take notes. Several students have no paper and pencil so he throws a tirade about the foibles of coming to class unprepared. He then reminds them that it is their responsibility to bring the proper supplies. After all, he is fulfilling his obligation by teaching the material. It is not his fault if they don't come prepared to learn it.

The lecture on dominant and recessive genes lasts for the remainder of the period but is interrupted periodically by Mr. Bledsoe's threats to several students who have decided that they will not comply with his many requests for them to stop talking and write. When the dismissal bell rings, students jump up and head for the door. Mr. Bledsoe makes them go back and sit down, reminding them that he dismisses them, not the bell. They then grumble that he is making them late for their next period class to which he replies, "It's your fault if you're late, not mine!"

■ SCENARIO II

Fortunately in every school there are teachers who effectively manage whichever students are lucky enough to be placed in their classrooms. Room 112 at John F. Kennedy Middle School is one such room, and Mrs. Dawson is one of those teachers.

Mrs. Dawson is short in stature, and most of the males in her history class tower over her; however, she is never heard speaking above a conversational tone. Mrs. Dawson is a proactive, brain-compatible classroom manager who plans bell-to-bell instruction for her middle school students daily. As students enter her class each period, she is standing at the door to warmly greet them. They hear classical music playing softly. Students have been taught how to talk beneath the calming music rather than over it. In fact, Mrs. Dawson spends a majority of her time during the first few days and weeks of school teaching her specific routines and procedures to each class. They then practice each ritual, such as when to talk and when not to, how to pass in papers, and how to move around the classroom for instructional purposes and get immediately back to their seats. She wants these routines to become so ingrained in students' brains that they become habitual.

Mrs. Dawson's room looks more like someone's home than the sterile, artificial environment of a classroom. Visualize this: The room has flexible seating with tables that seat four to five students. There are a few single desks dotting the landscape. In the back of the room are a sofa and a rocking chair for those students who may desire alternative forms of seating or need just a little more movement to facilitate their learning. The fluorescent lights in the ceiling of the room are turned off. The lighting provided is a combination of natural light from the windows on one side of the room and low lamp lighting on another. Since none of Mrs. Dawson's students has allergies, there is a distinct smell of lavender in her classroom, which has a calming effect on the brains of her students. There are pictures on the wall in support of the learning as well as a few pieces of art. There are also live plants scattered throughout the room. On Mrs. Dawson's desk are pictures of her family members, and on the wall beside her desk resides her degrees.

As students file into the room, they know to look for the sponge activity on the board. This activity absorbs precious drops of otherwise wasted instructional time and enables students to reconstruct or review content taught in a previous lesson. Sponge activities also help to ensure that they will remember important information not only for upcoming tests but for life. While this activity is being completed, Mrs. Dawson checks roll and class begins. Today, students will be working in cooperative groups to design a Civil War newspaper that depicts each group's understanding of the previously taught unit on the Civil War. Every group has been given a rubric that delineates exactly what each newspaper should include. According to the rubric, every group's newspaper should have a title, a cost, a motto, an index, a feature story with an accompanying image, several additional stories, an editorial, a crime story, and an advertisement. Students will spend the first few minutes of the period in their groups brainstorming possible ideas for their newspaper. The remainder of the period will be divided into two chunks: one featuring a mini-lecture accompanied by a graphic organizer, called a Venn diagram, comparing the Civil War and the Revolutionary War and a second chunk involving students in a Jeopardy game to review content prior to an upcoming test.

■ PROACTIVE PLANNING

Imagine that you're a teacher in a one-room schoolhouse in the 1800s. A student has aggravated you for the fifth time in the same day. You have had enough so you pull a revolver concealed under your jacket and demand that the student sit down or be buried in the schoolyard. The student promptly sits down.

Fast forward to the 2000s. A student has aggravated you for the fifth time in one day. You have had enough and demand that the student sit down or be sent to the principal's office. The student curses you, laughs, and continues his mischief.

What a difference between the two scenarios, and neither one is acceptable! Even in the early 1960s, the major disciplinary offenses involved talking too much in class, chewing gum, being out of seat, or throwing paper. Today teachers are dealing with students' inability to pay attention, refusal to complete assigned work, blatant disrespect, and violence against adults and other students. In fact, it is now the students who are concealing the weapons.

There is good news, however! Even in the current decade, there are teachers in every school who are exceptional managers of their classrooms. These teachers are proactive, not reactive, and use brain-compatible techniques and strategies to accomplish this feat. The research on classroom management tells us that effective managers do not necessarily possess this magic bag of tricks that other teachers do not have. Instead, they have planned for their students in ways that keep classroom management problems from happening in the first place.

Let's consider this real-world analogy to distinguish between the concepts of reactive and proactive planning. Suppose you visit a small town and notice that people are falling off a cliff when they come to the end of a certain unmarked road. The town council has two options. They can park an ambulance at the bottom of the cliff so that when people fall off, they will be rushed to the hospital in the swiftest time possible. However, a second and more viable option might be to put a plan in place so that people do not fall over the cliff at all, making the ambulance unnecessary. Effective managers seldom need the ambulance because they plan for students not to fall off cliffs or misbehave.

This book will outline 20 ways that proactive teachers can accomplish four purposes:

- Create a physical classroom environment conducive to learning that includes appropriate lighting, music, aromas, and seating
- Develop a proactive classroom management plan with appropriate rituals, celebrations, consequences, and parental support
- Deliver brain-compatible lessons that not only reduce behavior problems but increase academic achievement and make teaching and learning fun
- Deal with chronic behavior problems that are not alleviated by conventional classroom management practices

Create a Physical Classroom Environment Conducive to Learning That Includes Appropriate Lighting, Music, Aromas, and Seating

Many behavior problems can be alleviated by the way a teacher sets up the classroom environment. Chapter 4 is devoted to creating a brain-compatible classroom that encourages the calming effect of natural or low light and discourages the use of fluorescent lighting, which can have detrimental effects on the health of both brain and body.

Teachers can actually change the state of students' brains by the type of music they play. Certain types of music actually calm the brain down and place it in a state for learning. These types include some classical, jazz, New Age, Celtic, and Native American music. At other times, before students become lethargic, they need the uplifting, energetic tunes of a faster pace of music such as big band sounds, country and western, and Motown. Chapter 5 focuses on the impact of music on the brain.

Aromatherapy is big business due to the impact that specific smells can have on the brain. Lavender, vanilla, and jasmine are just some of the scents that can have a calming effect on brains, while peppermint, lemon, citrus, and cinnamon can assist students in focusing and becoming more energized. Although Chapter 7 will touch on this topic, teachers must be careful of the ill effects of certain aromas on those students who have allergies and may want to save the tips in this chapter for their homes where they can best relieve the stresses of the day.

Providing alternative seating such as tables and chairs, sofas, bean bag chairs, rockers, or placing carpet squares on the floor enables students to explore other options for seating rather than the rock hard desks that they are required to occupy for the majority of the day. Refer to subsequent chapters for additional research and activities that help a teacher minimize disruptions by the very atmosphere with which they surround their students.

Develop a Proactive Classroom Management Plan With Appropriate Rituals, Celebrations, Consequences, and Parental Support

When I was taught to manage students several decades ago, my classroom management plan consisted of many rules, harsh consequences, and few rewards. Even today, some teachers are searching for the most severe consequences in an effort to squelch the inappropriate behaviors they are seeing daily in their classrooms. While consequences are certainly part of any plan, they do not appear to be the most important part. In fact, if consequences are so effective, why do such a high percentage of convicted criminals reoffend within three years of their release from prison?

It appears to be the positive experiences between teacher and student that correlate to sustained improvements in student behavior. These include high expectations for student success, positive rapport between teacher and student, direct instruction in the appropriate expectations and procedures for effective functioning in the classroom, specific feedback regarding student responses, celebrations for improved student performance, low-profile interventions when students are off task, and, finally, appropriate consequences for more high-profile misbehavior. Specific chapters of this book are devoted to each of the aforementioned topics.

Once an effective management plan has been developed, it should be communicated to all stakeholders. Chapter 20 speaks to the importance of establishing year-long, proactive, and positive relationships with all of the adults in the lives of students.

Deliver Brain-Compatible Lessons That Not Only Reduce Behavior Problems But Increase Academic Achievement and Make Teaching and Learning Fun

Many instances of inappropriate behavior can be linked to students who are bored by the content or feel unable to accomplish the assigned tasks. They cover their inadequacy with misbehavior. A teacher's best line of defense against behavior problems is that teacher's ability to actively engage students in meaningful and relevant lessons. In the three bestsellers *Worksheets Don't Grow Dendrites: 20 Instructional Strategies That Engage the Brain* (2003), *Reading and Language Arts Worksheets Don't Grow Dendrites: 20 Literacy Strategies That Engage the Brain* (2005), and the adult learning text, *"Sit and Get" Won't Grow Dendrites: 20 Professional Learning Strategies That Engage the Adult Brain* (2004), I have identified 20 brain-compatible strategies that take advantage of the way the brain learns best. When students are actively engaged through the use of these strategies, the ones who were bored become interested and the ones who had feelings of inadequacy are learning, therefore minimizing classroom disruptions.

Although these 20 strategies will be referred to throughout this book as ways for maximizing classroom instructional time and minimizing disruptions, they are listed in their entirety below:

- brainstorming and discussion
- drawing and artwork
- field trips
- games
- graphic organizers, semantic maps, and word webs
- humor
- manipulatives, experiments, labs, and models
- metaphors, analogies, and similes
- mnemonic devices
- movement
- music, rhythm, rhyme, and rap
- project-based and problem-based instruction
- reciprocal teaching and cooperative learning
- role-plays, drama, pantomimes, and charades
- storytelling
- technology
- visualization and guided imagery
- visuals
- work-study and apprenticeships
- writing and journals. (Tate, 2003, 2004, 2005)

When you view the list you might initially assume that these strategies are best used at the kindergarten or lower grade levels. However, learning style theory (Gardner, 1983; Sternberg & Grigorenko, 2000) and brain research (Hannaford, 1995; Jensen, 1994, 1995, 1996, 2000a, 2001; Wolfe, 2001) relate that these strategies are just as appropriate for all grade levels and all content areas. They also address eight of Gardner's multiple intelligences and all four (visual, auditory, tactile, and kinesthetic) learning styles (see Table I). Even adult brains learn more if the recommended strategies are used to engage the brain (Tate, 2004).

When planning lessons, teachers should consult the list and select those strategies that would be most appropriate for teaching the specified objective. For example, consider the following sample lessons:

- When teaching the novel *The Giver*, students could participate in a teacher-led **discussion** of the following question: Is there such a thing as utopia?
- Students could **draw** a picture illustrating the definition of content-area vocabulary words.
- A teacher could formulate a Jeopardy **game** to review pertinent content prior to a test.
- Short mini-lectures could be accompanied by semantic, concept, or thinking maps or other types of **graphic organizers.**

- When teaching the concept of main idea, students could use the strategy of **metaphor, analogy,** and **simile** to compare the concept to a text message because both give just "the gist."
- Students could **move** to other students in the room who will serve as their energizing partners and use **reciprocal teaching** to relate a concept just taught.
- When teaching some geometric terms, students could move their arms to **role-play** the following: right angle, obtuse angle, acute angle.
- History teachers could tell **stories** to help their students recall pertinent historical events in chronological order.
- Students could do quick **writes** to recall cross-curricular content, for example: In less than two minutes, write three causes of the Civil War.

It was Aristotle who once said that one learns to do by doing. Thousands of years later, that concept still applies. The activity generated when students' bodies are talking and moving to learn content not only reduces behavior problems but increases academic achievement and makes teaching and learning fun.

Deal With Chronic Behavior Problems That Are Not Alleviated by Conventional Classroom Management Practices

No matter how proactive a teacher is, there may be some chronic behavior problems for which one cannot prepare. Being proactive, in this case, means becoming informed about those brains that may learn or behave differently from the norm and soliciting the help of others when that help is warranted. Chapter 19 provides a brief overview of such chronic behavior challenges as attention deficit disorder, learned helplessness, stress or anxiety disorder, oppositional disorder, and conduct disorder. Students who possess these different ways of behaving can be the greatest challenges for even the best classroom managers. However, the more a teacher understands the unique brains of these students, the more equipped that teacher is to formulate an arsenal of possible solutions to the puzzle these students provide. A summary of those solutions will be provided.

■ SUMMARY

When teachers are reactive, rather than proactive, behavior problems may truly upset them because they have not anticipated the problems and are not equipped with possible solutions. This stress or frustration may result in increased use of sarcasm, random punishments, and even shouting or yelling. But *Shouting Won't Grow Dendrites.* In fact, consider this simile: It has been said that shouting to manage students is like blowing the horn to steer a car. After all, excessive blowing of horns escalates road rage just like

Table I   Comparison of Brain-Compatible Strategies to Learning Theory

Strategies	*Multiple Intelligences*	*VAKT*
1. Brainstorming and discussion	Verbal-linguistic	Auditory
2. Drawing and artwork	Spatial	Kinesthetic/tactile
3. Field trips	Naturalist	Kinesthetic/tactile
4. Games	Interpersonal	Kinesthetic/tactile
5. Graphic organizers, semantic maps, and word webs	Logical-mathematical/ spatial	Visual/tactile
6. Humor	Verbal-linguistic	Auditory
7. Manipulatives, experiments, labs, and models	Logical-mathematical	Tactile
8. Metaphors, analogies, and similes	Spatial	Visual/auditory
9. Mnemonic devices	Musical-rhythmic	Visual/auditory
10. Movement	Bodily-kinesthetic	Kinesthetic
11. Music, rhythm, rhyme, and rap	Musical-rhythmic	Auditory
12. Project-based and problem-based instruction	Logical-mathematical	Visual/tactile
13. Reciprocal teaching and cooperative learning	Verbal-linguistic	Auditory
14. Role-plays, drama, pantomimes, charades	Bodily-kinesthetic	Kinesthetic
15. Storytelling	Verbal-linguistic	Auditory
16. Technology	Spatial	Visual/tactile
17. Visualization and guided imagery	Spatial	Visual
18. Visuals	Spatial	Visual
19. Work study and apprenticeships	Interpersonal	Kinesthetic
20. Writing and journals	Intrapersonal	Visual/tactile

excessive shouting at students escalates power struggles. In my observations, teachers who yell at students often have students who yell back, causing the teacher to yell even louder and the vicious cycle to continue.

Proactive classroom managers anticipate and prepare for the avoidance of behavior problems. They arrange their classroom to create a calming state for learning in the brains of their students. They run student-centered classrooms where relevant lessons are delivered using brain-compatible strategies. They build rapport with their students and their parents who all know that the teacher has each student's best interest at heart. Their class is perceived as a challenging but fun place to be.

When behavior problems occur, proactive teachers initially use low-profile interventions so that they can correct the misbehavior while continuing to teach. If a consequence is warranted, it is used as a last resort and implemented in a calm, caring manner that conveys the message that the student is respected even though the misbehavior will not be tolerated. In other words, as one band director told me, "I am the three F's."

I am firm (They know I mean what I say.)

I am fair (I am consistent every day.)

I am friendly (They know I care in every way.)

Acknowledgments

In every school I visit, there are teachers whose classrooms are very effectively managed and whose students excel at extremely high levels. What's more impressive is that those teachers accomplish this amazing feat without ever raising their voices. You see, they have already figured out that *Shouting Won't Grow Dendrites.* This book is dedicated to that group of teachers because the proactive management skills that they have already mastered will be reflected in the chapters that follow.

This book is also dedicated to those teachers who are striving daily to become better at what they do, for to never be satisfied with the status quo is to strive toward perfection. I pray that this book enables them to realize that the best-run classrooms are positive places to be, where teachers present challenging activity-based lessons and where students believe that academically all things are possible.

I also dedicate this book to my parents, Alvin and Eurica, who instilled in me and my two sisters the values and respect that are lacking in some of today's students. I will forever be grateful for the times we said, "No sir" to my father and "Yes ma'am" to my mother. Their highest of expectations equipped us with the confidence, skills, and abilities to be successful at whatever we undertook. I am attempting to do the same with my three children, Jennifer, Jessica, and Christopher.

To my husband, Tyrone: For 28 years you have been my confidant and best friend. Thanks for your continued love and encouragement, which enables me to perform at my best during every presentation.

Thanks to the associates who work with our company, Developing Minds, Inc. You are instrumental in spreading the word that all students can succeed. I am also grateful to Carol and Karen who *keep me straight* both professionally and personally.

Corwin Press gratefully acknowledges the contributions of the following reviewers:

Catherine Kilfoyle Duffy
English Department Chairperson
Three Village Central School District
Setauket, NY

Kathryn McCormick
National Board Certified Teacher
Gahanna Middle School East
Gahanna, OH

Kathie F. Nunley
Founder, Brains.org
Amherst, NH

Sue A. Delay
K–12 Curriculum Resource Teacher
Oak Creek-Franklin Joint School District
Adjunct Faculty, Cardinal Stritch University
Muskego, WI

Carol Gallegos
Literacy Coach
Hanford Elementary School District
Hanford, CA

Denise Leonard
Staff Development Resource Teacher
Torrance Unified School District
Torrance, CA

About the Author

 **Marcia L. Tate, EdD** is the former Executive Director of Professional Development for the DeKalb County School System, Decatur, Georgia. During her 30-year career with the district, she has been a classroom teacher, reading specialist, language arts coordinator, and staff development director. She received the 2001 Distinguished Staff Developer Award for the State of Georgia, and her department was chosen to receive the Exemplary Program Award for the state.

Marcia is currently an educational consultant and has taught over 125,000 administrators, teachers, parents, and business and community leaders throughout the world. She is a member of the Corwin Press Speaker's Bureau and the author of the following three bestsellers: *Worksheets Don't Grow Dendrites: 20 Instructional Strategies That Engage the Brain*, *"Sit and Get" Won't Grow Dendrites: 20 Professional Learning Strategies That Engage the Adult Brain*, and *Reading and Language Arts Worksheets Don't Grow Dendrites: 20 Literacy Strategies That Engage the Brain*. Participants in her workshops refer to them as "the best ones they have ever experienced" because Marcia uses the 20 strategies outlined in her books to actively engage her audiences.

Marcia received her bachelor's degree in psychology and elementary education from Spelman College in Atlanta, Georgia. She earned her master's degree in remedial reading from the University of Michigan in Ann Arbor, her specialist degree in educational leadership from Georgia State University, and her doctorate in educational leadership from Clark Atlanta University. Spelman College awarded her the Apple Award for excellence in the field of education.

Marcia is married to Tyrone Tate and is the proud mother of three children: Jennifer, Jessica, and Christopher.

1

Be Proactive, Not Reactive

WHAT: PLANNING IS THE KEY

Ineffective classroom managers wait until problems occur and then decide how they will deal with each situation. They are not consistent, and they dole out disciplinary consequences depending on their mood or their feeling for a particular student, usually with a great deal of screaming, shouting, or other negative emotions. They appear annoyed, frustrated, and often engage students in power struggles, which teachers are always destined to lose.

For example, several years ago I was observing in the classroom of a teacher who consistently experienced a large number of disciplinary offenses. Her students did not like her and the feeling seemed to be mutual. The teacher was walking up and down the aisles of the classroom and noticed the book bag of one of the students she liked lying in the aisle near the student's desk. She politely asked the student to pick up the book bag and place it in the appropriate location so that she would not trip over it. The student complied. Several weeks later, I was once again observing the same teacher when a similar incident occurred. However, this particular book bag belonged to a student who was one of her pet peeves. The reaction this time was totally different. She kicked the book bag while screaming at the student to get it out of her way. She then accused him of purposely trying to trip her. The student shrugged his shoulders but reluctantly moved the book bag while mumbling some indiscernible words under his breath.

The research that follows summarizes some of the key concepts of proactive management. Teachers who manage well are able to separate the behavior from the student. They are capable of putting proactive plans in place so that the majority of potential behavior problems never actually occur. They also use brain-compatible strategies that actively engage all students in the learning. Since the average attention span in minutes is approximately equivalent to the age of the student, proactive teachers divide the content into meaningful chunks or segments and then teach each chunk by allowing students to practice what they are learning through active engagement strategies. It is the purpose of this book in this and subsequent chapters to show the reader specifically how to be a more proactive and less reactive classroom manager.

1

WHY: THEORETICAL FRAMEWORK

Learning as much as you can about your diverse learners enables you to *bridge the cultural gaps* between you and them (Davis, 2006).

Because teachers will always have someone who may become a behavior problem, they must be both mentally and physically prepared for whatever happens (Crawford, 2004).

Taking advantage of students' strengths is a major way to decrease behavior problems and increase achievement (Davis, 2006).

Effective classroom managers will exhibit the following proactive characteristics:

- They lead the class by modeling the expected behaviors, such as how to control impulsivity and how to use positive self-talk.
- They build resiliency in students by gathering and interpreting student data, developing a positive relationship with each student, providing feedback to each student, understanding students' unique differences, and understanding that content should be taught from a variety of linguistic and nonlinguistic organizers.
- They take care of behavior problems quietly and quickly.
- They move from low-profile interventions to more elevated measures while remaining calm.
- They realize that student behavior can be affected by a positive physical and emotional environment.
- They provide routines that are followed consistently daily.
- They assist students in perceiving the value or importance of the task.
- They directly teach students how to reach personal goals and provide feedback on their progress toward those goals.
- They reduce stress by making sure that students know what to do and how to do it (Tileston, 2004).

Teachers should have very clear expectations of what will be acceptable as appropriate behavior and what will not be accepted (Crawford, 2004).

A smart teacher who is in tune with students will make changes before boredom or disinterest sets in (Tileston, 2004).

Because classroom management is tightly tied to how we deliver instruction, lessons that engage and motivate students minimize management concerns (Smith, 2004).

Because each student has a preferred modality, if a student does not understand a concept after the first presentation, the teacher should change to another modality when re-teaching that concept (Tileston, 2004).

Learning strategies with high degrees of inherent positive and negative feedback facilitate the learning process better than a *sit and get* lecture (Jensen, 2003, p. 28).

Brain-compatible strategies are research-based, are just plain common sense, and take advantage of the way students learn—which is why they work (Erlauer, 2003).

Change the state (feeling moments) of a student's brain and you will change his or her behavior. Social interaction, movement, music, and lighting variations all change the state of the brain (Jensen, 2003).

Students who are provided with enough time to process what they are learning not only retain their focus for a longer period of time but retain more of what is taught (DiGiulio, 2000).

Thanks to medical advances and amazing discoveries about how the brain learns, teachers now know why some methods work better than others (Erlauer, 2003).

Anticipate and prevent misbehavior before it occurs by thoroughly examining a specific situation and asking questions, such as What are the circumstances that could lead to an outburst or explosion? (Kottler, 2002).

Effective teachers plan backward by starting where they expect to end up (Guskey, 2001).

Once students' attention is captured, their interest can be maintained by using a variety of instructional approaches such as demonstrations, reviews, group projects, problem solving, role-playing, gaming, and computer-assisted instruction (Burden, 2000).

When students' brains are experiencing downtime, hands-on lessons will keep their brains alert and actively engaged (Erlauer, 2003).

When teachers instruct students in remembering information with words and images, they are using mnemonics (Carney & Levin, 2000).

Students who experience success seldom misbehave. To experience success a student must do something of value (DiGiulio, 2000).

Brain-compatible strategies can address the downtime within a lesson that occurs after approximately the first 20 minutes (Sousa, 2001).

A teacher's effectiveness for the remainder of the school year will be determined by what that teacher does during the first few days of school (Wong & Wong, 1998).

What a student does—participates, performs, creates, designs, produces—has a greater impact on a student's feeling of success than what the teacher believes, knows, or says (DiGiulio, 2000).

Ineffective teachers discipline their classrooms; effective teachers manage their classrooms (Wong & Wong, 1998, p. 83).

The most effective way to deal with misbehavior is to prevent the misbehavior in the first place (Burke, 1992).

HOW: CLASSROOM APPLICATION

• Many of your classroom management concerns can be alleviated by the way you set up the physical space around you. By arranging your classroom to facilitate the physical movement of students and to expedite their conversation about class content, a great deal of management concerns can be avoided. Turn the artificial environment of school into a homelike atmosphere by adding plants, alternative seating, and natural or low lighting. Consult Chapters 4 through 8 for specific suggestions that will enable you to create a brain-compatible, proactive classroom environment.

- Prior to the beginning of the school year, determine those rituals (expectations and procedures) that will be required of students to maintain appropriate discipline in your classroom. For example, since students need to talk, how will you get students' attention when you need it? Since students need to move, how will you get them in and out of their seats? (See Chapter 12 for ways to determine and teach your rituals.)

- When students' brains and bodies are actively engaged in learning, behavior problems are diminished. Those students who were bored become actively engaged. Students with feelings of inadequacy gain confidence. Plan to use the 20 strategies outlined in the book *Worksheets Don't Grow Dendrites: 20 Instructional Strategies That Engage the Brain,* which take advantage of the way brains learn best. When planning a lesson, determine the purpose of the lesson (objective, standard) and the knowledge and skill students should know and be able to perform. Examine the list of strategies to ascertain which one(s) would be most appropriate for delivering the instruction in a brain-compatible way. These strategies are outlined in the Introduction of this book.

- Prior to the beginning of the school year, make plans for ways to celebrate the successes of those students who are complying with classroom expectations and procedures. (See Chapter 16 for sample celebration activities.)

- Prior to the beginning of the school year, make plans for the negative consequences that students will encounter if they choose not to follow the established expectations and procedures. (See Chapter 18 for sample consequences for misbehavior.)

- Involve students in determining the classroom's rituals, celebrations, and consequences. When students have input into the development of a classroom management plan, they are more likely to take ownership of the plan and its implementation. In fact, students will often formulate plans that are stricter than the teacher's original ideas.

- Determine ways to remain calm when students disrupt or refuse to comply with designated expectations and procedures. These ways may include counting to ten, pausing, taking deep breaths, regarding the incident as humorous, or feeling confident that you can deal with the challenge at hand.

- Learn to separate the disciplinary infraction from the student. Maintain the utmost respect while informing the student that you will not tolerate this type of behavior in your classroom.

REFLECTION

> ## What is my plan for becoming a proactive, not reactive, classroom manager?

1. _____
   _____
   _____
   _____
   _____

2. _____
   _____
   _____
   _____
   _____

3. _____
   _____
   _____
   _____
   _____

4. _____
   _____
   _____
   _____
   _____

5. _____
   _____
   _____
   _____

2

Expect the Best!

WHAT: YOU GET WHAT YOU EXPECT

You may have noticed that in almost every school where students change classes there is a group of students who will be perfectly behaved in one classroom and out-of-control misfits in another. Why does this happen? It may have to do with teacher expectations. You get what you expect! Students tend to live up or down to the expectations afforded them. Effective classroom managers possess the highest of expectations for student success and put plans in place to ensure that those expectations are met.

The research on expectations started in the 1960s. It began in the experimental psychology classroom of Dr. Robert Rosenthal. Dr. Rosenthal's students were charged with the task of getting white mice to run a maze in the shortest time possible. He divided his class into an experimental and a control group. Students in the control group were told that their mice were regular, run-of-the-mill lab mice. Students in the experimental group were told that they had carefully bred, top-of-the-line mice and to expect great things of them.

The rest is a matter of record. The mice in the experimental group ran the maze three to four times faster than those in the control group. In fact, there was no difference between the mice in the two groups. They were just randomly assigned to the experimenters; however, the students in the experimental group used more motivating and supportive interactions, and look what resulted! You get what you expect!

Robert Rosenthal teamed with a researcher by the name of Lenore Jacobson to ascertain whether what worked in the laboratory would work in a school system. They told specific groups of teachers in the Los Angeles County school system that they were being given students who had been identified by a test as late bloomers and to expect great achievement from these students this particular year. Other groups of teachers were told nothing out of the ordinary. Well, you guessed it! The students whose teachers expected great things far exceeded those whose teachers did not have the same high expectations—not only on achievement tests but measures of aptitude as well. The study became the noteworthy *Pygmalion in the Classroom* (Rosenthal & Jacobson, 1992). You get what you expect!

"My teacher says I'm an underachiever, but I
think she's an overexpecter."

I realized several years ago that my sisters and I are products of high expectations. My parents and grandparents expected great things from us academically. They set the bar high and we exceeded it. Our father used to tell us that in school, the grade of "C" on a report card meant "fair" and that he was not raising fair children but exceptional ones. When three girls hear those words long enough over a stretch of years, they come to believe it. My older sister and I have earned doctorates, and my younger sister is the Human Resources Manager for the Atlanta Symphony Orchestra and its subsidiaries. Our teachers also expected great things from us and, as a result, classmates of ours became teachers, ministers, doctors, lawyers, and so on. You get what you expect!

Teachers who are exceptional classroom managers expect that their students will be well-disciplined and put a proactive plan in place to ensure that their expectations are met. You will never hear them make the following statements: What else can you expect from these kids? Johnny is disrespectful but he has no parental support and is doing the best he can! I have the worst seventh-grade class in the school! And guess what? These teachers get what they expect!

A time-tested program called TESA (Teacher Expectations and Student Achievement) delineates 15 interactions that teachers can practice to communicate the highest of expectations to their students. These interactions include who the teacher calls on to respond to questions or to participate in class, how much waiting time is allowed from the time a question is asked until an answer is expected, whether the teacher delves or assists students in coming up with the correct answer, where the teacher stands in the room, how courteous the teacher is, and how much personal interest the teacher takes in each student. More than 40 years of research show that when these 15 interactions are practiced with every student, amazing results follow. Academic achievement is increased for all students, absenteeism is reduced, and behavior concerns diminish. For more information on this Phi Delta Kappa sanctioned program, consult the Los Angeles County Office of Education at 1-800-566-6651.

WHY: THEORETICAL FRAMEWORK

Teachers with high expectations could be thought of as difficult or very demanding, but they feel the end result is worth it (Orange, 2005).

Intelligence that is learned is more strongly correlated to success in school than the intelligence with which we are born (Marzano, 2004).

When teachers expect positive results from their class, they will expend energy making those results happen. When teachers expect negative results, they expend just as much energy on failure (Wong & Wong, 1998).

Although many students come to school without the social skills, manners, and respect necessary for good behavior, proactive teachers expect that all students can be taught these behaviors (Burns, 2003).

High and low ability labels placed on first graders follow them through elementary and middle school (Johnson, 2002).

A teacher who is considered effective has three characteristics: (1) maintains positive expectations for the success of students; (2) is extremely effective at classroom management; and (3) is capable of designing lessons so that students master content (Wong & Wong, 1998).

Students will customarily rise to the expectations of their teacher (Burden, 2000).

It is possible for every student to learn on grade level, even those that other teachers have given up on (Johnson, 2002).

A teacher must exhibit positive expectations toward students because the research shows that whatever the teacher expects from the student is exactly what the student will produce (Wong & Wong, 1998).

One of four supportive interventions that allow students to learn and foster prosocial behavior is the teacher's ability to communicate instructional expectations for students (DiGiulio, 2000).

Labeling students with positive qualities while telling them how you expect them to act builds self-esteem and strengthens the relationship between teacher and student (Koenig, 2000).

People in the power structure of a society look for other people who resemble themselves, resulting in a closed system. Closed systems create a self-fulfilling prophecy (Sternberg & Grigorenko, 2000).

> Well-managed classrooms have four characteristics: (1) students who are intimately involved in their academic work; (2) students who know what the expectations are and are successful with those expectations; (3) very little confusion, few disruptions, and maximized instructional time; and (4) a climate that is task-oriented but pleasant and relaxed (Wong & Wong, 1998).
>
> Increasing the time that you wait for a student's response when you ask a question to an average of five seconds and accompanying that wait time with a higher-level question results in more thoughtful student responses (Cawelti, 1995).
>
> Teachers who tell students of their high expectations for success obtain greater increases in academic achievement than teachers who communicate low expectations (U. S. Department of Education, 1986).

HOW: CLASSROOM APPLICATION

• Find ways to communicate to your class that you have the highest of expectations for them. Tell them from day one of school that they are one of the smartest and most well-behaved groups of students you have had the pleasure of working with and that you will not settle for anything less. Refer to them as *bright, gifted, wonderful,* and *a joy to teach,* and mean it. Watch them live up to your expectations!

• Create the expectation that courteous behavior is the norm in your classroom, regardless of whether students practice courtesy outside of the classroom. Model courtesy at every possible moment. Use words like *good morning, please, thank you, I'm sorry, excuse me* with all students. Insist that students use the same courteous words with you and one another. Do not allow words of discourtesy such as *shut up, you idiot, talk to the hand, that's stupid,* and so on when students are in your classroom.

• Watch where you stand in the classroom. Effective teachers with high expectations *teach on their feet and not in their seats.* If you don't assign seats, you will find that students who feel good about their abilities will often choose to sit along the front row or in the middle of the room. Students who don't feel as capable will sit at the back of the room. Place yourself in close proximity to all students by walking the room. Stand near every student in the class at some point during the lesson.

• Being near students during independent seat work enables you to communicate your high expectations and provide students with individual assistance when necessary. A technique by Fred Jones (2000) called *praise, prompt, and leave* allows you to help more students in a shorter period of time. The three steps in this techniques are as follows: (1) When you look at a student's independent seat work, make a positive comment or *praise* statement about what has been done so far; (2) If there is an error, provide a clue or *prompt* to move the student in the direction of a better answer; (3) Then *leave* that student and move on to the next student. If the prompt in step two is not sufficient, assign a close partner or another student to work with the student needing the help. This frees you to quickly determine whether students actually understand or if reteaching is necessary.

• When a student misbehaves, label that student with a positive attribute and then state specifically what you expect of him or her, for example, "Kathy, you are a thoughtful person. I expect you to tell Sandra that you are sorry" (Koenig, 2000).

• Ask questions at all levels of Bloom's Taxonomy (n.d.) so that the expectation is communicated that all students are capable of answering both *easy* and *difficult* questions. As you teach and test, make certain to include questions from the knowledge, comprehension, application, analysis, synthesis, and evaluation levels. For example, let's take the story of *Goldilocks and the Three Bears.* A knowledge question would be "Which bear's chair got broken?" While there is nothing wrong with that question, it is the lowest level of the taxonomy. Higher-level questions would include the following: Place the events in the order in which they happened in the story (comprehension); Predict what would have happened if Goldilocks had been caught by the bears (application); Identify the theme of this fairy tale (analysis); Create a different ending to this story (synthesis); Defend Goldilocks's right to be in the home of the three bears (evaluation).

• I have taught classes in which I randomly called on a student and the student looked at me and asked, "Why did you call on me? I didn't have my hand raised." Communicate your high expectations to all students by creating the expectation that both volunteers and nonvolunteers will be called upon to participate. Use random ways of involving students such as writing their names on popsicle sticks or index cards, placing those sticks or cards in a can or box, and pulling a student's stick or card whenever a question is asked or involvement needed. Some teachers use a computer program that randomly flashes students' names on a screen.

One teacher I observed made a BINGO board out of her classroom by having students sit in five straight rows with five students in each row. Instead of using the word BINGO, she used the word LEARN. Therefore, if a student was sitting in Row 1, Seat 3, that student was in seat L3. At the front of the room was a canister containing the chips of all the seats in the room. Whenever student involvement was needed, the teacher reached in, pulled out a chip, and the chip designated the student who would respond. How motivating this method of participation was for this seventh-grade class!

• One of the major reasons that students are hesitant to respond in class is their fear of being embarrassed. From day one of school, establish the expectation that no student in class will be put down because of an incorrect answer. Tell students that our purpose in being in school is to learn and, in some cases, to learn from our mistakes. Tell them that some of the greatest inventions started out as mistakes. Examples would be the formula for Coca Cola or the Post-it notes that are used throughout the world. Set an example by never using sarcastic language or demeaning gestures with students. Remember, only 7% of your message comes from the words you say; the other 93% comes from your nonverbals (body language, gestures). In addition, don't allow students to ridicule or demean one another when an error is made. Establish your classroom as a community of learners.

• One of the reasons for students' incorrect answers is an inadequate amount of time between the time a teacher asks a question and the time the teacher expects the answer. Research shows that if teachers have high expectations they will wait approximately 2.6 seconds, but if teachers have low expectations they will wait less than one second (Kerman, 1979). Provide a minimum of five seconds of quiet from the time you ask a question until the time you expect an answer. Allowing more time for thinking results in more comprehensive answers and an expectation that all students are capable of giving quality responses.

• When a student answers a question incorrectly, or not at all, provide wait time as outlined above. If the student's answer is still inappropriate, rephrase the question, provide additional information, or give clues to move the student in the direction of the right answer.

REFLECTION

> ### What is my plan for communicating my highest expectations to all of my students?

1. _____
 _____
 _____
 _____

2. _____
 _____
 _____
 _____

3. _____
 _____
 _____
 _____

4. _____
 _____
 _____
 _____

5. _____
 _____
 _____
 _____

3

Understand the Symptoms

WHAT: CAUSES OF MISBEHAVIOR

Patrick is constantly calling your name. Even when he knows the answers to questions, he needs your assurance that his answers are correct. You are sick and tired of reprimanding him for talking out loud without being called upon first.

Melissa is demanding and argumentative. If you say the sky is blue, she says it's brown. She is always calling her peers inappropriate names and when reprimanded shrugs you off and refuses to listen to your requests.

Duane is bored with school and with you. He is frequently caught sleeping in class or at the very least with his head on his desk. He is unmotivated and puts out little effort. When not sleeping, he is looking for ways to bother the other students so that they cannot complete their assignments either.

When you give Gail an assignment, all you hear is "I don't understand," or "I can't do this!" She makes little effort and has literally given up. She is having great difficulty reading the grade level texts yet does not qualify for any special programs.

When students refuse to complete assigned tasks, disrupt your class, or are disrespectful to you and others, you may be tempted to treat the symptoms with the harshest of penalties. While there certainly should be consequences for misbehavior, effective classroom managers look beyond the symptoms to find the causes of the disruptions.

There appear to be four major reasons for student misbehavior: desire for attention, desire for control, boredom, and feelings of inadequacy. Let's examine each cause independently.

1. Some students need your attention and the attention of their classmates as well. For whatever reason, they get the idea that they are either being ignored or are not receiving the percentage of your time

that they feel they deserve. Therefore, they will call your name a hundred times a day, tap their pencil repeatedly, or disrupt other students who may be trying to do as you have requested. When they have gotten on your last nerve, you may be tempted to engage them in a power struggle or order them out of your classroom. Did you know that negative attention is considered better than no attention at all? Therefore, even if you argue with them or banish them to another location in the building, they have received the attention they seek. After all, every student in your class is giving them undivided attention as you administer your consequences.

2. A second reason that students misbehave involves their need for control. Many of your students have an inordinate amount of control in their homes. They may be raising younger brothers and sisters as well as themselves and, as a result, are *calling the shots* and making major life decisions. Then they come to school and cannot understand why

"No wonder I'm failing math. I'm just no good with numbers. Even when I dialed the math homework helpline, I got the wrong number. "

everyone, including you, will not dance to their music. The opposite also exists. Some students feel that they have little or absolutely no control over their personal lives; therefore, these students exhibit characteristics of belligerence, disrespect, and downright disobedience.

3. Other students misbehave because they are just plain bored. In many classrooms, students sit for long periods of time without any active engagement of their brains. Their brains are not getting enough oxygen and they may either yawn repeatedly, fall asleep, or think of other things while the lesson is being taught. They may also randomly hit a classmate simply because they cannot think of anything better to do, or because they would like to inject a little excitement into their day.

4. The fourth reason students disrupt has to do with their feelings of inadequacy. They really cannot do what you are requesting of them. Their brain does not have the confidence to believe that they are capable of being successful on the assigned task; therefore, they do things to divert attention away from their poor performance. After all, it is better to be considered the class clown than the class dummy. No one wants to be considered inadequate.

You can deal with difficult students if you first recognize their primary needs (Canter & Canter, 1993). Once you look beyond the symptoms of misbehavior, you may discover the causes. Simply treating the symptoms may stop them temporarily. However, if there is to be meaningful behavior change, a deeper inspection is warranted.

WHY: THEORETICAL FRAMEWORK

Students who need attention are often either kinesthetic or visual learners who do not learn best when the instruction is predominantly auditory (Tileston, 2004).

When students act out, it is often a call for help. When teachers understand and address these calls, they provide students with the best opportunities to make meaningful changes in behavior (Smith, 2004).

In order to be successful with students who are challenging, teachers must understand what is happening in their lives and the reasons behind why they act as they do (Kottler, 2002).

Attention-getting behavior can be addressed in the following ways:

1. Tell students precisely what the misbehavior, is, the consequences for the misbehavior, and why the consequences apply;

2. Use humor when talking with them about their misbehavior;

3. Negotiate with them by assuring them that you will incorporate movement and opportunities to talk with their classmates at the culmination of every teacher-directed segment;

4. Provide chances for students to move during the learning (Tileston, 2004).

Since boredom gets more students in trouble than almost any other misbehavior, teaching students *boring skills,* or what to do when they become bored, helps them to cope (Divinyi, 2003, p. 76).

The ways we interpret students' behavior make some students more difficult to manage than others (Kottler, 2002).

When students are bored, they often demonstrate off-task or attention-getting behavior (Tileston, 2004).

The following five reasons related to teacher planning may be taken into consideration as to why students misbehave:

- Students are bored due to lack of challenge in the lessons.
- Students quit due to feelings of their inability to complete the assignment.
- Students see lessons as irrelevant to their interests.
- Students can't follow the lesson due to disorganization.
- Students don't feel that the teacher cares for, likes, or respects them (Kottler, 2002).

When students seek attention, teachers feel annoyed. However, when students seek power and control, teachers feel threatened (Tileston, 2004).

Natural disasters and tragedies, transitions, unhealthy family situations, lack of parental discipline, marital discord, and disagreements within the family are all home and life factors which can increase in-school behavior problems (Kottler, 2002).

HOW: CLASSROOM APPLICATION

- Get to know each of your students personally in an effort to understand why they behave as they do. Begin with those students who may appear to give you more of a challenge than others. Once you comprehend what some of your students are experiencing, you may become more sympathetic to their challenging behavior and comprehend why they act as they do.

- Students who seek attention need attention. However, give them the attention when they are doing what is expected of them. Provide them with special recognition when you see them meeting expectations. Compliment them in front of their peers, write positive comments on their papers when their written work shows improvement, provide them with privileges that indicate growth. In the case of middle or high school students, special recognitions may be given in a private, rather than public, setting.

- Providing students with choice can give them some measure of control. Allow them to choose among several options for completing an assignment or responding to an assessment task.

- Students who seek control need to be given it. Put these students, along with others, into positions of responsibility. Make them line leaders, cooperative group facilitators, and peer teachers. With your supervision, allow them to teach a lesson to the class. You may very well have to equip them with the social skills necessary to get along with peers because many students who seek control exhibit few interpersonal skills. See Chapter 12 for specific directions on teaching your social skills to students.

- By using the 20 brain-compatible strategies outlined in the best-seller *Worksheets Don't Grow Dendrites: 20 Instructional Strategies That Engage the Brain* (Tate, 2003), students in your classroom will become actively engaged in learning. When they have opportunities to role-play vocabulary words, move to meet with a discussion partner, complete a project, or play a content-related game, students do not have time to be bored, and their behavior naturally improves. These strategies appear to work for all student populations including gifted, regular education, special education, and English as a Second Language students.

- Students who believe themselves to be inadequate need confidence. Often these students develop major behavior problems because they cloak their inadequacy with inappropriate behavior. Give these students successful experiences by providing work at an appropriate instructional level. As they begin to experience success, they will want to take on more challenging assignments. The 20 strategies mentioned above are the best way to increase understanding and retention of information for all students, including those performing significantly below grade level.

As a reading specialist, I often worked with students who were considerably below grade level in reading performance. They felt totally inadequate to deal with grade level text. I had to begin by teaching them at their instructional level in an effort to instill confidence in their ability to read. As the students experienced success, their brains gained confidence. It was amazing how quickly we progressed through more challenging material.

I cannot figure out how some teachers get the mistaken idea that if a student has a history of failing grades, he or she will be somehow motivated by receiving one more grade of "F" in the current class. There is nothing brain-compatible or logical about that concept at all.

- Refer to Chapter 19 for additional recommendations appropriate to those students who are in need of attention, power, or who feel inadequate.

REFLECTION

> **What is my plan for meeting the needs of each**
> **of the four types of misbehavior in my classroom?**

Goal: Attention _____

_____

_____

_____

_____

Goal: Control _____

_____

_____

_____

_____

Goal: Boredom _____

_____

_____

_____

_____

Goal: Inadequacy _____

_____

_____

_____

_____

4

Light Up
Their World

WHAT: LIGHTING AND THE BRAIN

A school system was in the process of building five new schools to house their increasing student population. Having read the research on the detrimental effects of fluorescent lighting, I shared with the architects rationales for including additional windows or a different type of lighting in the construction of these new buildings. The experts thanked me for my input but proceeded to include fluorescent lighting in plans for each of the five new edifices. You see, this type of lighting is less expensive. While fiscal responsibility is certainly warranted, the increased expense may be offset by decreases in misbehavior and ill health and increases in academic achievement.

The information I shared with the architects included the facts that fluorescent lighting pulses or flickers, which some students and adults can sense. This type of light tends to make hyperactive children more hyperactive, increase the onset of migraine headaches, and can cause those who are prone to epileptic seizures to experience an increase in the frequency and severity of those seizures.

More than 50 years ago, an extensive study of 160,000 students showed that when lighting in classrooms improved, so did student difficulties with vision, nutrition, infections, posture, and fatigue (Harmon, 1951). Additional neuroscientific research (Heschong, 1999; Jensen, 1995; MacLaughlin, Anderson, & Holic, 1982) reinforces the fact that the best light for the brain is natural light. It stands to reason that if the purpose of the brain is to help the body survive in the world, then natural light, such as sunlight, would be optimal. If your classroom has windows, open the shades and let the light shine through.

There are classrooms where windows are simply not an option. In fact, more and more schools are being built without windows. If this is the case in your environment, try bringing alternative lighting or lamps into your classroom. Even turning off half the fluorescent lights and supplementing with lamps is helpful. This practice alone appears to reduce behavior problems because the lower lighting calms the brain—a preferable state for optimal learning. In fact, lamps also give the classroom a homelike atmosphere, which is more natural for brains.

Fifteen percent of the population is impacted by Seasonal Affective Disorder (SAD), which is a form of depression that results when people are deprived of daylight for long periods of time. The symptoms usually disappear during the spring and summer months. Cognitive problems that may accompany SAD include lapses in verbal and visual memory and lack of attention (Michalon, Eskes, & Mate-Kole, 1997).

At home when you want to relax and block out the stresses of the day, try another type of low lighting—candlelight. Candles create a brain-compatible atmosphere conducive to calming and can make for a romantic evening. Why do you think I've been married for 28 years?

WHY: THEORETICAL FRAMEWORK

Avoiding fluorescent lighting and combining natural (sunlight) and indoor light is best for learning (Tileston, 2004).

Sunlight can freshen the dark sections of a room (DiGiulio, 2000).

Inadequate or inappropriate lighting, air, and heat can influence behavior (Tileston, 2004).

Fluorescent lights possess a flicker and barely discernable hum which can raise cortisol (stress hormone) levels and negatively impact the central nervous system of students (Jensen, 2000a).

A tri-state study of 21,000 students suggested that classrooms with large windows and a great deal of natural light produced students who scored 20% higher in math and 26% higher in reading than those with less lighting (Heschong, 1999).

Bright fluorescent lights appeared to create restless, overactive learners while lower-level lighting appeared to calm students (Jensen, 1995).

Ultraviolet light, which humans acquire from the sun, helps the body synthesize vitamin D. Vitamin D, in turn, assists the body in absorbing necessary minerals, and lack of these minerals can contribute to deficiencies in the nonverbal cognitive area of the brain (MacLaughlin et al., 1982).

Allow students to choose where they sit in class because many may be underachieving due to the effects of lighting on their eyes (Jensen, 1995).

A large number of students are more focused, more relaxed, and have better performance in classrooms with lower-level lighting (Krimsky, 1982).

HOW: CLASSROOM APPLICATION

• If you have windows in your classroom, let in the sunshine. It will provide your students' brains with the best source of lighting.

• If your classroom has fluorescent lighting with two separate light switches, turn off half the fluorescent lights and supplement with lamps.

This procedure will reduce the impact of a detrimental light source and provide a lower, softer source of illumination.

• If you only have one switch to your fluorescent lights, turn it off and bring lamps into your classroom. Certain types of floor lamps may have several separate light sources and can be directed to different areas of the room, thereby providing illumination to more students. If lamps do not provide sufficient lighting, explore the possibility of unscrewing the bulbs in half of your fluorescent lights and using a combination of both ceiling lights and lamps.

• Several teachers that I have observed allow their students to wear baseball caps in class to deflect the negative effects of fluorescent lighting. The bill of the cap causes the light to be deflected and not shine directly into the student's line of vision. Students are only allowed to wear the caps in class but must remove them before going into the hall or cafeteria.

• During the months with the least sunlight, convene some classes outdoors so that students can take advantage of the natural ultraviolet light from the sun.

• When students are not getting a sufficient amount of light and you are unable to take them outside, allow them to engage in movement connected to learning and other types of physical activity in the room. The activity will produce positive chemicals in the brain, such as epinephrine and dopamine, which can combat depression.

• Get your brain in a state of calm by relaxing with candles at home. Candlelight in combination with appropriate music and aromas will reduce stress and create an atmosphere conducive to relaxation. After all, a stress-free good night's sleep helps to prepare both brain and body to be a successful classroom manager on the following day.

REFLECTION

**What is my plan for providing
appropriate lighting in my classroom?**

1. _____

_____

_____

_____

2. _____

_____

_____

_____

3. _____

_____

_____

_____

4. _____

_____

_____

_____

5. _____

_____

_____

_____

5

Let the
Music Play

WHAT: MUSIC AND THE BRAIN

I simply cannot teach or live without music! Neither should you. Music gets each day off to an encouraging start, leads students calmly through transition times, minimizes classroom disruptions, and gives all who hear it a sense of well-being. Bringing the right kind of music into your classroom can alleviate at least 50% of your classroom management concerns.

In perusing the research on the power of music to affect the brain, you will find three major concepts. First, there tends to be a correlation between a person's ability to solve problems, particularly in mathematics, and his or her ability to play a musical instrument (College Board, 2000; Covino, 2002). My daughter, Jessica, is an example of this fact. Jessica took piano lessons for eight years, played the trombone in the band, sight reads music, and sang in both the chorus and chamber chorus in college. She also obtained a very high score on the mathematics portion of the Scholastic Aptitude Test (SAT) and speaks German fluently. I do believe that all the years of music training strengthened the spatial part of her brain that enabled her to excel at the higher levels of math and fluently speak a second language.

The second advantage of music lies in the fact than music helps you remember (Feinstein, 2004; Jensen, 2001; Sprenger, 1999; Webb & Webb, 1990). If you don't believe that music facilitates memory, you will not be able to complete this phrase. I bet you can do it! Fill in the blank: Conjunction junction, _____. If you answered, "What's your function?" then you are like the millions of people who were taught by the cartoon characters and catchy tunes of *Schoolhouse Rock*. I learned more English and history watching that show on Saturday mornings than I learned in my elementary and high school classes. Music is still being used today to teach students to remember content and is one of 20 strategies that I have identified as correlating with the way brains learn best.

However, the best use of music for classroom management is for calming students down and getting their brains in a state for learning (Erlauer, 2003; Sousa, 2001). The old saying, music hath charms to soothe the savage beast, is not only true, it is pervasive. I have experienced many classrooms, at all grade levels, in which students enter each morning or every period to some type of calming music playing softly in the background. Calming music includes some forms of classical, jazz, New Age, Celtic, or spiritual such as Native American flute music. Students can be taught that if their voices can be heard over the music, then they are talking too loudly.

Many school personnel have forbidden students to talk in the cafeteria. Names are taken and students pay harsh penalties all in the name of silent lunch. While you might disagree with this statement, I will make it anyway. I have come to the conclusion that it is unnatural to eat lunch with someone and not desire to talk with them. If the purpose of the brain is to survive in the world, then when is the last time that you went out to lunch or dinner with a friend and were not allowed to talk to them? Are we expecting behaviors of students that would not be characteristic of or appropriate for adults?

A better plan would be to have some type of calming music playing softly in the cafeteria throughout the lunch period and to have teachers

"I downloaded music from a radio station in South Korea, and I got Seoul music."

instruct their students in the proper voice tone and etiquette one should use when dining with friends. In this way, they would be equipping their students with lifelong skills for success.

Music can also change the state of the brain to one of enthusiasm and motivation. Visualize how engaged one gets when hearing the popular theme from the movie *Rocky.* I received an e-mail from an art teacher who related the following incident. He had attended one of my workshops and was having a difficult time getting his art students to clean up following the completion of their art projects. He found himself shouting at students to get the classroom cleaned up prior to the ringing of the bell each period. After hearing about the motivational aspects of music, the teacher decided to have students clean to the melodic rhythm of the song *Car Wash* by Rose Royce. What a difference! Students were now competing to be the first to finish cleaning before the song ended each period.

An assistant principal related this second scenario to me. Following her attendance at my workshop, she recommended that music be played in the halls of her building prior to the beginning of each school day. By the time "My Country 'Tis of Thee" ends, all students must be in their homeroom classes. She was amazed to see high school students scurrying down the hall to get to class prior to the culmination of the song. The assistant principal related that the tardy rate has dropped by 80% since the theme music was implemented.

As a rule of thumb, use music no more than one-third of the class period. Any strategy used continuously loses its novelty.

WHY: THEORETICAL FRAMEWORK

Music strengthens learning because it can have an amazing emotional impact on the brain (Tileston, 2004).

Music enables students to make personal connections with the content because it causes them to express emotions ranging from love, triumph, and hope to despair, anxiety, and fear (Feinstein, 2004).

Teachers should play music when they are not lecturing because background noise keeps students from feeling the need to create it themselves by talking (Crawford, 2004).

Music that gradually slows down has a comparable relaxing effect on the brain (Erlauer, 2003).

Music is a powerful tool for building emotions and strengthening memory (Feinstein, 2004).

A student's body will get in sync with the rhythm of live music played close by (Erlauer, 2003).

When students are talking with one another and brainstorming ideas, they should not have to compete with song lyrics. For most activities in the classroom, instrumental music should be used; however, music with lyrics can be used during transitions, special celebrations, or during games (Jensen, 2003).

Music awakens the brain and assists the student in maintaining interest (Sousa, 2001).

Specific areas of the brain, which are involved with emotion, actually show increases in activity when various pieces of music are played (Wolfe, 2001).

Studies suggest that playing background music in the classroom may help to improve the concentration of students while they are completing specific tasks (Sousa, 2001).

Music at 110 to 160 beats per minute will gain an increase in a person's heart rate and result in an increased state of arousal (Barlett, 1996).

Music has the therapeutic benefits of relieving the effects of stress, treating severe disabilities as well as visual and hearing defects, and boosting children's immune function (Sousa, 2001).

Using rhythm as a teaching strategy enables African American students to use a call-and-response pattern found in Black music (Nieto, 1999).

HOW: CLASSROOM APPLICATION

• Begin a collection of music of a variety of genres (classical, jazz, Celtic, big band, etc.). CDs with collections of music from the 60s, 70s, and 80s are particularly effective because the tunes are catchy and the majority of the lyrics are not objectionable.

• As your students enter your room each day or each period, have some type of calming music playing to get their brains in a state for learning. Teach them that as they assemble, their voices should not be heard over the music. Role-play the appropriate way to talk while listening to music, and have your class practice this skill until they get it right. Classical, smooth jazz, Celtic, Native American music, and nature sounds all tend to be calming for most brains.

If you do not wish to be charged with the responsibility of turning on the music daily, assign this task to a student whose sole job is to be your disc jockey for the week. Students could take turns with this task and may even wish to bring in appropriate music for the class to hear.

Don't be surprised if students object to the introduction of types of music to which they are not accustomed, such as classical or jazz. Teachers relate, however, that if they persist in their use of music, any day that they forget to turn it on, students will ask for it.

• Use energizing music when you want to invigorate, energize, or actively engage your class. Music with an upbeat tempo will wake up those brain cells and get the oxygen and blood pumping. This type of music can be playing while students are walking around the room in search of a partner with whom to discuss content or completing a high-energy activity such as drawing or using manipulatives. Country and western, rock and roll, folk tunes, polka, flamenco, and big band sounds will all fit the bill for a more energizing type of music.

• Select songs that fit the content of the unit of study. Music can peak interest and minimize behavior concerns. For example, when studying a period of history, play samples of accompanying music from that period. Play the theme from *Welcome Back, Kotter* to greet students following a long weekend or a holiday.

• Use music to assist you in setting time limits on assigned activities. For example, students must complete an activity by the time a specific song ends. Watch how motivated students become when trying to beat the music.

• Allow students to work individually or with peers to create a song, rhyme, rap, or poem that demonstrates their understanding of content. This is an engaging way to have students mentally rehearse what is taught.

• Celebrate academic and behavioral successes in your classroom with appropriate music. Songs like *We Are the Champions* by Queen, *Celebration* by Kool and the Gang, and *I Got the Power* by Snap all get students' brains fired up and excited when good things happen as students acquire new concepts and score well on measures of assessment.

• Consult the extensive list of calming and energizing music on pages 194–196 of Eric Jensen's book *Tools for Engagement* (2003).

• Remember that the majority of class time (approximately 60% to 70%) is spent without music. If music is played as students are writing or concentrating, keep the volume low so as not to disturb their thought processes. Be aware of students who have difficulty concentrating when there is any music played at all. In this case, music may be played only during transition times or headphones used by students who need them.

REFLECTION

> **What are the most appropriate times**
> **for incorporating music into my classroom?**

_____

_____

_____

_____

_____

_____

> **Which musical selections will I use?**

Calming

_____

_____

_____

_____

_____

High-Energy

_____

_____

_____

_____

_____

6

Color Their World

WHAT: COLOR AND THE BRAIN

Have you ever stopped to think about how the colors in this world affect you? I didn't think much about it until I made a mistake with color in my home. My husband and I dined with friends who had just moved into a beautiful new house. Their dining room was painted a cranberry color that provided an elegance to the already exquisite surroundings. We were so enamored of the wall color that we went home and painted the walls in our den the same color. For us this was a definite mistake! While cranberry was surely appropriate for the high-energy dining room in the home of our friends, it was not as applicable for the high ceilings in the den of our home. You see, the den had always been a calming place for the family to be. It was suddenly transformed into a high-energy room where no one chose to be anymore. Even our three children were not sitting in the den. We hastily repainted our den a hunter green, and everyone in the family returned to what had at one time been our favorite room in the house.

Not too long after this incident, I began reading brain research that explained exactly what had happened. Educators are only beginning to comprehend what people in advertising have known for a long time: that color influences emotion, behavior, mood, and even cognition (Jensen & Dabney, 2000).

I learned that reds (even cranberry), oranges, and deep yellows are high-energy colors for the brain. This is why most of the fast-food restaurants, such as Kentucky Fried Chicken and McDonald's, are painted these colors. I have even noticed that on the television weather forecast that when there is a preponderance of intense weather such as rain or wind, the color on the map where the weather is most severe is red, next severe is orange, and so on. Another example would be the correlation between the "terror alert" levels in the United States and the high-energy colors. When the alert levels are high, the color code is orange. When the threat level is lower, the corresponding color changes to yellow or green. This brings us to the consideration of the effect of color on the brain.

Since the brain was designed to exist in the world, wouldn't it make sense for the colors in nature to be the most calming colors for the brain? For example, the sky is blue, the grass is green, the earth is brown, and the rainbow is pastel. Therefore, blues, greens, earth tones, and pastels are among the most calming colors for each brain. The house that we live in now is very brain-compatible. Each room is a different shade of beige or brown, and no matter what room we are in, we experience a sense of satisfaction and peace. After all, I learned my lesson regarding color the hard way!

Color can even be beneficial for some readers. Colored overlays placed on top of an assignment or a book that a student is reading can be beneficial for those who experience what the research calls *scotopic sensitivity.* According to Rickelman and Henk (1990), this practice can provide many at-risk students with the chance that they need to be successful. In one research study, after only one week, those students who read with an appropriate colored transparency placed on top of their reading gained 6.6 months in reading achievement and 19.35 months in comprehension (O'Connor, Sofo, Kendall, & Olsen, 1988). These transparencies are usually light blue or yellow in color.

WHY: THEORETICAL FRAMEWORK

Underlining key words and important concepts with colored markers improves semantic memory and visual recognition (Jensen & Dabney, 2000).

Preschool students who experienced wall colors that appealed to them as well as other positive environmental changes cooperated more after their exposure than before (Read, Sugawara, & Brandt, 1999).

Writing in the color blue tends to provide a calming effect, which enables the brain to concentrate and think deeply (Wallace, West, Ware, & Dansereau, 1998).

The more colorful the imagery is when we initially experience a task, the more easily we can use similar images when we attempt to recall the learning situation at a later time (Jensen & Dabney, 2000).

Writing in the color red encourages high energy in the short term and inspires creativity (Wallace et al., 1998).

When college students took their mid-term exams on blue paper, their performance scores were higher than those students who took the same test on red paper (Sinclair, Soldat, & Mark, 1998).

The emotional responses of children to bright colors became more positive as they grew older, especially in the case of girls (Boyatzis & Varghese, 1994).

Over 40 years ago, it was found that the warm, shortwave colors of red, orange, and yellow tended to arouse people even if they didn't appear pleasing. The cool, long-wave colors of blues and greens tended to have a more calming effect on people (Shaie & Heiss, 1964).

HOW: CLASSROOM APPLICATION

- Use high-energy colors such as red, orange, or deep yellow to motivate or excite students. Many primary classrooms are replete with colorful rugs and bulletin boards that catch the eye of the students and create an air of excitement in the room.

- Use calming colors such as blues, greens, pastels, or earth tones to create a more relaxing classroom atmosphere.

- Blue dry erase or permanent markers are preferable for writing on the board or on a flip chart.

- When grading papers, use more calming markers such as blue or green to make comments or correct mistakes. Red tends to be more alarming and offensive to the brain, particularly when it is coupled with negative remarks or recommendations.

- Have students who need them place light yellow or blue acetate sheets on top of their stark white paper when reading. Some students have improved focus and reading performance when looking through colored sheets.

- Place colored markers or pencils on the school supply list for your students. Have them use these markers or pencils to underline important concepts or key words and phrases in their notes for emphasis. Color will call attention to crucial notes and make them more memorable to the brain.

- Thinking, concept, mind, or semantic maps are types of graphic organizers that appeal to both left and right hemispheres of the brain. They are pictorial representations of linear ideas. Adding color to these mind maps only increases their effectiveness and impact on students' comprehension and retention. Markowitz and Jensen (1999) describe the four steps involved in creating a mind map:
    o Get a large sheet of paper and colored markers;
    o Draw the central topic or main idea on the paper;
    o Add lines coming out of the central topic to depict key ideas or subtopics;
    o Make it personal by doodling, illustrating, or using symbols to assist the brain in recalling the information.

- Have students add color to their computer graphics, reports, presentations, and projects for increased appeal and better retention.

REFLECTION

> ## What is my plan for incorporating appropriate color into my classroom?

1. _____

_____

_____

_____

2. _____

_____

_____

_____

3. _____

_____

_____

_____

4. _____

_____

_____

_____

5. _____

_____

_____

_____

7

Stop and Smell the Roses

WHAT: AROMAS AND THE BRAIN

Have you noticed that when you smell a particular odor memories come flooding back? Maybe it's a scent from your childhood that brings to mind your mother cooking one of your favorite foods in the family kitchen. Maybe it's a fragrance that a particular person wears, and, when you smell it, all of the memories of your experiences with that person are recalled.

Your sense of smell is the sense most strongly related to memory. People are keenly aware of the circumstances associated with smells. Did you know, however, that certain smells can calm the brain, others can excite or invigorate the brain, while still others have the ability to improve concentration and memory?

Before we begin this discussion, be aware that certain students in your classroom may have allergies. You will not want to do anything to cause a student to become uncomfortable or to aggravate his or her allergies. Therefore, take this fact into consideration when using aromas in your classroom. If you do have such a student, then use the information regarding aromas to make your house a more inviting place. That is exactly what I did.

When I worked in the Department of Professional Development with the DeKalb County School System, I had a metal ring placed on a light bulb in my office. I poured lavender oil into the metal ring. Whenever I turned on that lamp, the light bulb would heat the metal ring, sending the aroma of lavender into the air. Lavender has a very calming effect on the brain, so the combination of classical music played on my CD player, low lighting, and a rock garden in the corner made my office a calming and brain-compatible place. People would come into my office and not want to leave. However, the lavender bothered the allergies of a person in my department so I discontinued its use, although I do have ceramic pots in every major room in my house. I place a tea light in the bottom of the pot and a lavender tart in the top. As the tea light melts the tart, the aroma of lavender pervades my house and calm takes over my body. The stresses of the day all seem to melt along with the melting of the lavender tart, which, by the way, can be used repeatedly.

WHY: THEORETICAL FRAMEWORK

When considering aromatherapy for the mind, try rosemary for enhanced alertness and mental clarity or a basil oil to get rid of mental fatigue and increase the brain's ability to pay attention and focus. Lemon or peppermint tends to be effective for energizing the brain (Nargundkar, 2001).

Adding a scent of lemon to the classroom helps to involve all of the senses in the learning experience (Feinstein, 2004).

Aromas should be used in early childhood programs to create the proper atmosphere. Peppermint, cinnamon, and orange make children more alert. Lavender, rose, and chamomile calm them down. These aromas can be added to play dough or paints and placed in potpourri bags around the classroom but out of the reach of the children (Schiller, 2001).

A human being's sense of smell is crucial because it is one of the most direct pathways to the brain (Dhong, Chung, & Doty, 1999).

Natural, everyday odors affect our mood, sleep patterns, cognition, and how productive we are (Pauli, Bourne, Diekmann, & Birbaumer, 1999).

In learning environments where lavender was used, students performed better (Schnaubelt, 1999).

Patients with brain injury performed as well as healthy patients in a test of vigilance following sporadic squirts of peppermint (Sullivan, Schefft, Warm, & Dember, 1998).

After smelling the scent of vanilla, undergraduate psychology students performed better in word naming and association (Pauli et al., 1999).

Production workers tested on their degree of vigilance (necessary for professions such as air traffic controllers) showed a 15 to 20 percent improvement in performance when they received a peppermint odor every five minutes (Dember & Parasuraman, 1993).

Lemon fragrances were used to increase concentration and attention in college undergraduates (Engen, 1991).

Students' sense of smell is linked to both the brain's frontal lobe, where problem-solving and planning occur, and to the limbic system, where emotion and memory are housed (van Toller, 1988).

HOW: CLASSROOM APPLICATION

• Poll your class to ensure that students are not allergic to specific fragrances. If any student falls into that category, you will have to use the information in this chapter in your personal, rather than professional, life.

- Use peppermint scents to energize students late in the school day. Thyme and rosemary are also energizing fragrances.

- Use lavender, jasmine, vanilla, or chamomile to calm the brains of students and reduce stress. Calming fragrances paired with calming music can relieve a large percentage of your discipline concerns.

- If you have students who are allergic to certain fragrances and you, therefore, cannot place them in the room for all to smell, purchase a *car jar*. Car jars are individual packets of specific aromas that students can smell, but the fragrance is not pervasive enough to cover the room. Place the car jar at one place in the room (away from any student who is allergic), and allow students to get up one at a time and take a sniff when needed.

- Eliminate unpleasant odors; they tend to negatively impact learning.

- Following a busy or stressful school day, use lavender, jasmine, or vanilla plug-ins at home to relax.

- Another aromatherapy technique, which can be used at home, consists of placing a tea light in the bottom of a ceramic pot and placing a tart on the top of the pot. As the pot heats, the tart melts, putting the energizing or calming fragrance in the air. This technique works well if there is a great deal of room area to cover at home.

- Tarts, oils, and scents can be purchased at any bath and body shop or online.

REFLECTION

What is my plan for incorporating appropriate
aromas into my classroom?

1. _____

   _____

   _____

   _____

2. _____

   _____

   _____

   _____

3. _____

   _____

   _____

   _____

4. _____

   _____

   _____

   _____

5. _____

   _____

   _____

   _____

8

Create a Natural Environment

WHAT: ROOM ARRANGEMENT AND THE BRAIN

Your brain has but one purpose: to help your body survive in the "real" world. Notice that I said, "in the real world." In the real world, the body is not confined to a wooden or metal desk five to six hours per day. It is allowed to sit and stand and bend and flex and recline and lie down, but this is not so in most classrooms. You see, school is a very artificial place for both brain and body. Recess and nap time are even being taken away from little ones in the name of increased time on task and academic achievement. In many classrooms, older students sit in uncomfortable desks unless it is time for lunch, physical education, or a change of classes. We often wonder why boys, particularly, are out of their seats or leaning with one knee in the desk and the other foot on the floor. Perhaps boys are even more uncomfortable with continuous sitting than are girls, but they do not want to be in trouble for being out of seat.

When I teach staff development classes, adults will often come up before class and ask my permission to stand or take breaks during instruction due to recurring back problems or other health issues. I always consent because I want my adult learners to be as comfortable as possible. What if I responded to their requests with the comment, "You must stay in your seat during instruction. I am sorry about your health issues." Do you think their brains would be in much of a state to hear what I had to say following that response? I think not!

As long as students do not infringe on the rights of their peers, they should be offered flexible seating options. What would be wrong with offering students multiple opportunities to move while learning? In fact, moving places the information in one of the strongest memory systems in the brain—procedural memory (Jensen, 2003; Sprenger, 2002). See Chapter 14 for additional research on the benefits of movement for the brain. When students must be seated, why not provide some alternatives to desks such as tables and chairs, carpet squares on the floor, an old discarded sofa, or an occasional bean bag chair. What would be wrong with letting students stand for short periods? As a fourth-grade teacher, I had a podium in the back of my classroom so that if a student needed to stand and write, he or she could take the opportunity to do so. Some teachers provide rocking chairs for those attention deficit disordered students whose brains might appreciate a little extra movement.

Different seating arrangements can provide novelty to the brain. Students can be shown how to move their seats into different configurations, depending on what the subsequent activity requires. Once shown, they should practice seat rearrangement until they can move them quickly and quietly. In addition, having students move to various locations in the room during instruction facilitates episodic memory because the brain not only remembers what it learns, but also where it was when it learned it.

Since brains were meant to exist in the real world and not an artificial place called school, the closer the classroom can come to a homelike environment, the better. Some middle and high school classrooms have

**"To maximize classroom instruction,
the Feng Shui consultant advises
one student desk per classroom."**

very little on the walls. Images on the wall can be very effective supports for learning and give students something relevant to look at when their attention to direct instruction wanes. However, balance is necessary. Too much on the wall can overstimulate students, especially students whose brains have difficulty focusing and paying attention.

Adding plants can help with needed oxygen. Family pictures on a teacher's desk can help students realize that they are being taught by a real person with a life outside of the school day. Proactive managers plan their classroom environment so that students have an atmosphere most conducive to positive thinking and long-term retention.

Providing some seating alternatives for students will not increase your classroom management concerns, as some teachers might expect. If the movement is structured and organized within the context of the lesson, this technique will actually reduce the number of behavior challenges. Students will learn with more comfort and their brains will simultaneously produce dopamine—the neurotransmitter that assists them in focusing and paying attention.

WHY: THEORETICAL FRAMEWORK

Changing room arrangement following a unit of study strengthens the episodic memory pathway, which attaches the student's learning to the context in which it was acquired (Tileston, 2004).

Considerations for room arrangement include the following:

- Can students move without running into each other?
- Are students close enough to the front of the room?
- Are students close enough to share the learning but far enough apart not to be distracting?
- Can the teacher easily circulate among student desks?
- Can all students see the teacher and the board?
- Do students have easy access to frequently used materials?
- Are there homelike touches in the room such as plants, lamps, etc.?
- Are visuals on the walls simple but related to the learning?
- Does computer placement facilitate a calm learning environment? (Smith, 2004)

Good room arrangement should facilitate both student and teacher movement, support successful classroom management and student achievement, and facilitate meaningful connections between students and their teacher (Belvel & Jordan, 2003).

Having students move their own chairs into different configurations keeps them curious and anticipating the next class activity (Jensen, 2003).

Five benefits of good room arrangement are as follows:

- Enables students to feel safe and secure
- Reduces the number of distractions
- Provides a smooth flow of students and materials
- Supports more attention to time on task
- Allows for all students to have access to the teacher (Belvel & Jordan, 2003)

Students' desks should be arranged so that the teacher can be seen during either whole class or small group instruction, but high-traffic areas should be kept clear (Wong & Wong, 1998).

Seating should be consistent with the activities being implemented, such as straight rows for direct instruction and desks in small groups for cooperative learning or small group activities (Smith, 2004).

Arrange the room so that needed materials are easily accessible and student materials are easily stored via boxes, dishpans, trays, and so on (Wong & Wong, 1998).

The seating can be rearranged to match the chosen activities as long as the students have mastered the procedures for moving their desks (Smith, 2004).

While an effective teacher assigns students to their seats on the first day of school, a teacher's major focus should be the facilitation of the instructional program (Wong & Wong, 1998).

HOW: CLASSROOM APPLICATION

- Find ways to engage students' bodies while learning. They could be role-playing an event in history or acting out a vocabulary word. There are multiple opportunities to engage both brain and body in the act of learning.

- Arrange your classroom to provide some alternate forms of seating. Bring in an old sofa, a rocking chair, a bean bag chair, or carpet squares so that students could sit on the floor with a partner and complete an assignment.

- Rather than desks, request tables and chairs so that the strategy of reciprocal teaching or cooperative learning is facilitated. This type of seating makes it easier for students to talk with a partner or a group or "family" of peers when necessary.

- Place a podium or stand in the back of the classroom so that hyperactive children (or those who just need a break from sitting) can write and participate while standing.

- Teach students how to move their chairs into different configurations to facilitate various learning structures such as pairs for reciprocal teaching or groups of four or five to facilitate cooperative learning. Have them practice this ritual until it becomes habitual.

- Find reasons for students to add oxygen and blood to their brains simply by standing while learning. For example, they could be on their feet while discussing information or reteaching a concept just taught to a peer. When teaching the difference between common and proper nouns, they could remain seated when a common noun is named and stand every time a proper noun is named.

- Have students change their episodic memory by changing their location in the room. If you are not comfortable with students constantly changing seats, then have them stand and review a concept just taught by moving to another area of the room.

- In addition to flexible seating, give your classroom a more authentic look by including either live or artificial plants, an aquarium, pictures on the walls, and personal artifacts that symbolize your life such as pictures of your family, degrees earned, and so on.

REFLECTION

What is my plan for incorporating alternative seating and natural artifacts into my classroom to make it more authentic?

1. _____

_____

_____

_____

2. _____

_____

_____

_____

3. _____

_____

_____

_____

4. _____

_____

_____

_____

5. _____

_____

_____

_____

9

Keep Them Laughing

WHAT: HUMOR AND THE BRAIN

A cartoon was shown of a classroom where students were literally hanging from the ceiling, tied by their feet. Outside the door there was a sign that read, "In-school suspension." This cartoon shown in a workshop on classroom management practically ensures a chuckle or two. That chuckle goes a long way in creating a climate conducive for learning. Tempers can be cooled and showdowns often avoided when a teacher employs the age-old strategy of humor.

Laughter has been called *internal jogging* because it can have as beneficial an effect on the brain and body as traditional jogging and aerobic exercise. When students are learning content by participating in motivating simulations, when there is *feel good* music playing in the background, and when students are *jogging internally,* the positive environment so essential for retention of information is created.

Humor can also result from students' involvement with games. I play Jeopardy with students and adults to review course content. They work in teams with a spokesperson who selects answers from various categories connected to the content being reviewed. The team then works together to provide the appropriate questions to the answers on the board, much the same way as contestants do during the television show. I even have the music for Jeopardy, which I play throughout the game show and I call myself Alicia Trebek, the female counterpart to Alex. Students love it and laugh the entire time. Other games such as ball toss, *Wheel of Fortune,* and *Who Wants to be a Millionaire?* add excitement to what could be an otherwise boring lesson.

Eric Jensen (1998) suggests that middle or high school teachers appoint a class clown whose job it is to tell a riddle, pun, or joke at an appropriate time. (This activity is outlined in another section of this chapter.) After the class has worked hard and when their brains need some down time, have the student tell the joke. Students will laugh, thereby facilitating memory and creating a positive classroom climate conducive to learning.

Don't ever confuse humor with sarcasm. Any statement that demeans or dehumanizes a student destroys the emotional support that so many students come to school needing. I have often heard teachers say, "When I am sarcastic, my students like it. They understand me and they even laugh!" Ask yourself this question: What else are they going to do? Students have to save face in front of their peers, so even if they feel humiliated, they may not admit it to you. Then, consider this scenario. When the teacher says something sarcastic to a student, what if that student comes back with a sarcastic statement to the teacher? That student will probably be ordered out of class and to the office or, at the very least, reprimanded for disrespectful behavior. If you expect respect from your students, you must model it with your students.

WHY: THEORETICAL FRAMEWORK

Optimism, the expectation that things will ultimately be all right, protects students from lapsing into hopelessness or depression when times are tough (Tileston, 2004).

Since the language skills of older adolescents are more highly developed, they can understand the subtlety of humor, irony, or satire (Feinstein, 2004).

Keeping a sense of humor enables a teacher to appreciate the creativity in the funny and weird things that some students do (Kottler, 2002).

A class that laughs together bonds and develops a spirit of community, which leads to a positive classroom suitable for learning (Sousa, 2001).

Cortisol, the stress hormone, can impact short-term memory or the brain's ability to organize and remember information (Feinstein, 2004).

Laughter causes the body to release natural pain killers called endorphins. These help both body and mind enjoy the moment (Sousa, 2001).

Games, simulations, and other entertaining and fun activities capture students' attention in the lesson (Burden, 2000).

Humor lessens stress and mental and physical tension, thereby shortening the school day (Burgess, 2000).

A smile or even a humorous comment directed at the situation can defuse potential misbehavior and lay the groundwork for defusing future problems (DiGiulio, 2000).

Fun is one of five crucial needs that must be satisfied if students are to be effectively motivated. The others are the need for survival, belonging and love, power, and freedom (Glasser, 1999).

Displays of humor not only help students feel better but result in increased attention and recall of information (Shammin & Stuss, 1999).

A student's creativity and productivity is increased by humor (Feigelson, 1998).

Performance and memory are improved when the classroom is a positive experience (Pert, 1997).

HOW: CLASSROOM APPLICATION

• Buy a joke book and start your class with a joke of the day. If you tell a joke at the beginning of each period and students begin to look forward to it, they will be sure to show up on time for your class. After all, who wants to miss out on an opportunity to laugh?

• Appoint a *class clown* whose job it is to tell a joke at an appointed time during the day or period. Have the student tell you the joke prior to class to make sure that it is appropriate for students. Jokes can put students' brains in the right frame of mind for learning and contribute to a positive classroom environment (Jensen, 1998).

• Have students place appropriate jokes or riddles on cards and bring them to class. Put all of the cards in a box and have a student draw one card out daily. Share the joke with the entire class.

• Find cartoons that can accompany the content that you are teaching and share them with the class at the appropriate time.

• Find a joke or cartoon and read it aloud to the class, omitting the punch line. Have students work on their inference skills by attempting to supply the missing punch line.

• As a sponge (warm-up) activity, have a riddle on the board when students arrive for class. Students may work individually or in teams to attempt to solve the riddle. They may turn their answers in on paper, and at the end of the class period or the week, the answer is revealed. Riddles not only provide fun and challenge but encourage higher level thinking and reasoning.

• Have students bring in editorial cartoons to share with classmates. Encourage them to use their higher level thinking skills to explain the reasoning behind the design of the cartoons.

• Have students design their own cartoons, comic books, or superheroes to illustrate key concepts taught. For example, in science class, students could design a comic book in which the main character is Molecule Man, a superhero with all the strengths and powers of a molecule.

• Play games to review content prior to a test. When many brains hear the words "Let's play a game!" those brains say, "Oh, goody!"

• Appreciate the creativity and comical lengths certain students go to in order to entertain themselves. Do as one teacher did. Keep a journal of all the weird and funny things students do in order to get attention in your classroom. When you take a step backward, you will begin to appreciate how truly creative they can be (Kottler, 2002).

REFLECTION

> **What is my plan for incorporating humor into my classroom?**

_____

_____

_____

_____

_____

_____

_____

> **List below the punch lines of jokes and/or the answers to riddles that you would like to incorporate.**

_____

_____

_____

_____

_____

_____

_____

10

"Hook" Them In

WHAT: ATTENTION AND THE BRAIN

You might think that when students are sitting quietly and looking at you, you have their undivided attention. Let me tell you something you probably have already figured out. Students can be looking dead in your face and not paying a bit of attention to what you are saying. Just because you have their eyes doesn't mean that you have their brain. In fact, the average attention span for listening to a lecture is commensurate with the age of the student. For example, a 6-year-old appears able to listen without active engagement for about six minutes, a 12-year-old, twelve minutes, and so forth. However, the maximum amount of time, even for an adult, is approximately 20 minutes. After that time, without active engagement, the brain has simply had enough (Tileston, 2004).

Even within the aforementioned time parameters, teachers stand a better chance of capturing students' attention if they utilize any one of four *hooks* for the brain: need, novelty, meaning, or emotion. In fact, behavior problems are minimized when teachers have the full attention of students during a lesson. Television and movie producers know the power of the *hook.* How many times have you been watching a show or a movie in which something occurred during the first few minutes to hook your attention? For example, during the show *Seinfeld,* Jerry Seinfeld always opened with a stand-up comedy routine related to the topic of the show. Steven Spielberg opened the movie *Jaws* with a scene in which a woman swimming alone is attacked and killed by a great white shark.

Teachers are also entertainers whose job is to capture the interest of their audience. What better way to do that than with the four engagement hooks: need, novelty, meaning, and emotion. Let's consider each one separately.

Need

Have you ever learned something because you simply needed to know it? Need is a useful way of getting and keeping the brain's attention. People learn what they need to know when they need to know it. Most human beings today don't even see the need to memorize telephone numbers if those numbers can be programmed into their cell phones. They will memorize a number when the information cannot be retrieved any other way. Convince students that they need the information that you are teaching and they will more than likely pay attention to it.

To establish students' need for what you are teaching, give them a purpose for learning it. Open your lesson with a reason why the particular objective you are teaching is necessary to master. For example, if I am teaching students a lesson on cause and effect, I would tell them that everything that happens in life appears to have a cause and every cause tends to have an effect. Tell them that if you are aware of the causes and effects of events, then you can predict what may occur.

Sometimes teachers will tell me that they truly cannot think of a reason that students need to know what they are teaching. You know what my next question to them is. Then why teach it?

Novelty

If need will not work for your lesson, the next hook is novelty. The brain also pays attention to things that are new or different. Novelty is a

"How come the History Channel is so interesting and my history class is so boring?"

motivator that can be easily incorporated into a teacher's lessons. Let me tell you a short story. (There I go using one of the 20 strategies that take advantage of the way brains learn best: storytelling.)

For 17 years, I lived in a subdivision across the street from a railroad track. When we first moved in, I could hear the train every time it came down the track. That lasted less than a month. Soon the noise of the train was not novel anymore, and I rarely paid any attention to the train's scheduled runs. This story is analogous to what happens in a classroom when students come to expect lessons presented in the same way day after day—through boring lectures or numerous worksheets. Soon they, too, are not paying attention anymore.

Why not add a little novelty into your lessons each day so that students never know exactly what to expect in your lesson presentation? In fact, while your classroom rituals and procedures should remain constant, your lesson should not. The 20 brain-compatible strategies outlined in the Introduction of this book should serve as vehicles for a never-ending supply of novelty. For example, I teach nine different professional development classes. Each one is novel. I use different music, games, stories, and so on to maintain the interest of those teachers who have taken several different classes from me. Just visualize how many different stories you can tell, movements or role-plays that your students can perform, songs you can sing, or projects in which your students can engage. While there are only 20 strategies, there are an unlimited number of ways to utilize them.

Meaning

A third way to gain students' attention is to connect the learning to real life. It stands to reason that if the brain was meant to survive in the real world, then the closer a teacher can get the instruction to the real world, the more memorable it becomes. Here's a real-life example. My daughter, Jessica, had been studying German in college and learned a great deal from the classes she took. However, it was not until she spent a summer interning and living in Germany and taking courses at the University of Berlin that she really began to apply and internalize what she had been learning in that artificial place called school.

For a primary classroom, counting money doesn't mean anything until we set up a classroom store and buy and sell goods that cost the amounts that students are trying to learn. Percentages don't mean a thing until you tell students that after today's lesson, they will be able to approximate how much money they can save when they see a percent-off sign on any item in the store. When students can see the connection between what you are teaching and their world, attention is increased. However, you have to know something about your students' lives to appropriately connect what you are teaching to their world. Refer to Chapter 11 for additional information regarding the importance of relevance to the brain.

Emotion

The final motivator for capturing attention is emotion. Of all four, it is possibly the most powerful. Anything that happened in the world or in your personal life that was filled with emotion tends to be unforgettable. I bet you can even remember what you were doing on January 28, 1986, when you heard that the *Challenger* shuttle had exploded in space. Even though that was over 20 years ago, most people have no difficulty recalling where they were because that day was filled with emotion. After all, even a teacher was on board.

Capitalize on this aspect of the brain by emotionally connecting your students to the content. For example, I walked into the room of a middle school teacher and immediately noticed an empty refrigerator box in the corner of the room. This box must have been novel to the students filing in because each one asked the teacher what the box was doing there. The teacher just told all of the students to put their books down and step in the box. Pretty soon I decided to join the 24 sixth graders who were jammed into the cardboard container. When the last student had entered the box, the teacher announced that they had just experienced what it must have been like for the Jewish people to be jammed into boxcars on their way to the concentration camps during the Holocaust. Every student was now emotionally connected to her subsequent lesson and they were hooked. The room was so quiet that you could hear a proverbial pin drop. I still get goose bumps when I retell this lesson opening.

Teaching with a passion or love for your content also emotionally connects you with students and students to the lesson. Do you remember teachers who were so enthusiastic about their content that their enthusiasm became contagious—a math teacher who made you love math, a science teacher who instilled in you a curiosity about the world? Emotion, then, becomes a powerful motivator.

What about the flip side of emotion? What about the students who enter your room daily with brains in such a state of high stress that they cannot think? While you may be able to do little to reduce the stresses of your students' personal lives, your classroom might be the one bright spot in their otherwise dismal day. Make your classroom a positive place to be emotionally and the learning will follow. While low to moderate stress can be good for learning, the brain learns best when it is not in high stress!

WHY: THEORETICAL FRAMEWORK

The brain likes novelty because whatever the brain perceives as unusual wakes it up and causes it to produce norepinephrine (Sprenger, 2005).

You have to capture students' attention before you can maintain it, and using novelty is one way to capture it (Feinstein, 2004).

Whether or not students pay attention is determined by the attitudes, emotions, and beliefs of their *self-system* (Tileston, 2004).

If teachers don't get the attention of students, the hope that they will remember any of the lesson is extremely remote (Feinstein, 2004).

Since our attention to and perception of an event are affected by emotion, emotion can be used to make teaching and learning more memorable (Sprenger, 2005).

Changing the pace of a lesson or the voice tone, moving around the room, using color markers or chalk, or bringing additional items into the classroom are all ways to integrate novelty into the lesson (Feinstein, 2004).

The four components of a student's self-system are as follows: (1) importance or relevance; (2) efficacy or the student's belief that he or she can actually accomplish the task; (3) emotional response, which can either hinder or enhance learning; and (4) motivation, which is a combination of the previous three components (Tileston, 2004).

By committing to change what you do and how you do it, you maintain your excitement for what you are doing (Kottler, 2002).

When teachers are excited about their subject matter, their excitement is contagious (Lewis, Amini, & Lannon, 2000).

A teacher's job is to increase student interest because it is known that when students are interested in a task they will love doing the task and perform it for a longer period of time (DiGiulio, 2000).

HOW: CLASSROOM APPLICATION

• Your students' brains are motivated by information that is needed to survive in the real world. Open your lesson by telling students why they need the information or skill you will be teaching. For example, when teaching students how to calculate simple interest, tell them that they need this skill so that they will be able to transact a loan for their future car.

• The brain pays attention to things that are novel, or new and different. Keep novelty alive in the classroom by changing things in the environment such as rearranging student desks, bringing in plants, or introducing different types of music in support of the lesson.

• Dressing in a novel way, moving around the room, or changing the pace of the class or the tone of your voice are other ways to maintain students' attention (Feinstein, 2004).

• Changing students' location in the room is a way to give them a fresh and different perspective. In fact, simply having students learn something in one location in the room and review it while sitting in a different location places the information at two different sites in the brain, enabling students to recall it from either place.

- The best way to keep novelty alive in the classroom is to vary instruction using the 20 brain-compatible strategies outlined in the Introduction. While it is important to maintain consistent classroom rituals and procedures, it is equally important to use a variety of methods for delivering instruction. This way, students come to class excited because they never know what to expect. For example, when teaching vocabulary, have students role-play the definition, illustrate the meaning, visualize the word connected to its definition, or write a song that symbolizes the concept.

- Relevance is a key component in understanding and retention. When students can see the connection between what they are learning and their world, retention improves. Therefore, always use real-life examples to illustrate points being made in a lesson. For example, when teaching students to solve word problems, I never begin with the problems in the math text. I use the names of students in the class and make up original problems based on actual events in their lives. In a recent lesson on elapsed time, the class and I discussed how much time had elapsed from the time Shawn (a student in class) got up until the time he caught the school bus and until the time he arrived at school. Content is far more meaningful when real-life examples are used as illustrations.

- Emotion is an important way that the brain stores information. Anything emotional that happened in your personal life or in the world at large is long remembered. For example, in the opening of one lesson on the Holocaust, show poignant scenes from *Schindler's List*. In another lesson, don't tell students what concept you are teaching, but make alarming statements about teenagers as soon as they get in the classroom. When students are really upset, announce that they have just experienced the negative effects of *propaganda*. You'll have their attention.

- Teach your content with enthusiasm. Show passion and love for the subject you teach, and that passion will become contagious. There is nothing better for maintaining the attention of students than an interesting lesson taught by a motivated teacher. After all, one of the major reasons students disrupt is boredom.

REFLECTION

What is my plan for gaining and maintaining students' attention in a lesson?

---

*In which lessons can I use **need** to get students' attention?*

_____

_____

_____

_____

_____

_____

*In which lessons can I use **novelty** to get students' attention?*

_____

_____

_____

_____

_____

_____

*In which lessons can I use **meaning** to get students' attention?*

_____

_____

_____

_____

_____

_____

*In which lessons can I use **emotion** to get students' attention?*

_____

_____

_____

_____

_____

_____

11

Make Learning Relevant

WHAT: CONNECTING TO REAL LIFE

How many times has a student asked you, "Why do we have to learn this?" That student was probably not being facetious and should not be penalized for sarcasm. If the purpose of the brain is to survive in the world, when students cannot see the connection between the lesson being taught and their world, the question will be asked. The answer is simple. Show the student the connection between what you are teaching and their world.

For example, if I were teaching elementary students the concept of main idea and details, I could use the simile of a table top and legs. I would open my lesson with the following *hook.*

> Class, look at the table in our classroom. The top of the table is supported by the four legs. A main idea in a story we will read must also be held up, or supported, by the details in the story. Let's draw a table with four legs. When we discover the main idea, we will write it on the top of our table. Then, we will find four supporting details to hold up that main idea and write one detail on each leg of our table.

A middle or high school lesson on main idea might open with the following *hook.*

> Class, how many of you have sent a text message to a friend on your cell phone? Well, today we are going to discuss why you need to recognize and form a main idea statement. You see, when you text message a friend, you are actually giving them the main idea, or gist, of your message. You cannot give them more of the details because that would be too expensive. Today, we are going to read several paragraphs and then stories where the main idea, or text message, is stated and we have to find it. Then, we will get so good at this concept that we will be able to formulate our own main ideas. We will then text message our original main ideas to one another.

With this opening to my lesson, I stand a better chance of attracting the attention of most, if not all, of my students and decreasing disruptions or classroom management concerns.

In the book *Worksheets Don't Grow Dendrites* (Tate, 2003), all 20 strategies work for the brain because they represent the ways in which human beings acquire and retain information. Several of the strategies, however, relate directly to relevant learning. They are as follows: field trips; manipulatives, experiments, labs, and models; project-based and problem-based instruction; technology; and work-study. Let's examine the relevance of each of these strategies.

When students take field trips they are able to travel to real places relevant to the content being studied. Even some of the greatest teachers in the world, such as Socrates and Aristotle, used the field trip as a major instructional tool (Krepel & Duvall, 1981). Take the field trip closer to the beginning of the unit of study so that the real-world connections can make the learning more comprehensible and memorable. In this day and age, teachers have an additional option: to take virtual field trips via modern technology.

When students use manipulatives, build models, perform experiments, or conduct labs, they are using their hands to connect with the world. This is why students often count on their fingers before they count in the abstract. A chemistry student who may have difficulty passing an objective paper-and-pencil test may well be capable of conducting the labs required for the course. These labs will help the student experience what real chemists actually do. Isn't it strange that in many classrooms throughout the country, lab work only counts for 20% or less of the overall grade, when real chemists spend more time performing labs than anything else?

Conducting real-world projects and solving real-life problems encourage active learning and discourage student passivity (Silver, Strong, & Perini, 2000). In fact, I bet you still remember a project in which you were engaged when you were in school. I still remember securing some water from the creek across the street from my house, bringing it to school in a baby food jar, and placing a drop of it under the microscope so that we could look for paramecia. When students solve problems, they also perceive the curriculum as more relevant.

The U.S. Secretary's Commission on the Acquisition of Necessary Skills (SCANS, 1991) report lists the ability to use technology as one competency that high school students must possess if they are to be prepared for the world of work. While the use of technology is a viable vehicle for effective instruction, using it as the sole means is problematic. The SCANS report also lists interpersonal skills as an essential competency. It is difficult for students to develop the essential social skills needed in the workplace if they are not provided with opportunities to do so in class. Another reason for the use of more active engagement strategies stems from the fact that as students sit in front of the computer, video games, and television, they develop a more sedentary lifestyle. As a result, the incidence of Type 2 diabetes is increasing at an alarming rate.

Work-study, apprenticeships, practica, and internships are viable tools for actively engaging students in meaningful and relevant curriculum, diminishing the number and frequency of behavior problems. Even in alternative schools throughout the nation, where student populations consists of those who have been suspended or expelled from traditional schools due to severe disciplinary infractions, work-study appears to be the order of the day. When I teach in these schools, I observe students involved in planting and tending gardens or preparing and serving meals. All students benefit when the academics are integrated into the relevant world of work.

WHY: THEORETICAL FRAMEWORK

For students to be motivated, they must perceive the subjects taught in school, such as reading, math, history, and science, as either necessary or desirable (Sprenger, 2005).

When students are actively engaged in art or science projects, problem-solving activities, and role-plays or simulations, they strengthen the thinking skills contained in the cerebellum (Feinstein, 2004).

The chances that new information will be remembered are increased when that information is connected to relevant issues (Sprenger, 2005).

Students disengage from learning when they do not perceive the relevance of it, are bored by it, or become stressed with it (Tileston, 2004).

Giving consideration to students' interests helps to guarantee that they can apply the standardized content they are learning to real life (Feinstein, 2004).

Students' self-systems (their attitudes, beliefs, and emotions) are directly influenced by their belief that the knowledge they are about to learn or the tasks they are about to complete are relevant to them and important to know and be able to do (Tileston, 2004).

When we impart information to students, their brains attempt to connect the new information to patterns previously stored. When there are no such connections, the new information can be lost (Sprenger, 2005).

Have students set personal goals for their learning and inquire often to make sure that they are meeting those goals (Tileston, 2004).

Relevance, high interest, choice, and authenticity are crucial criteria in motivating young adolescents (Beamon, 2001).

School-to-career initiatives allow students to successfully transition to the real world of work because they make school experiences relevant (Thiers, 1995).

HOW: CLASSROOM APPLICATION

• Open your lesson by telling students what they will be taught and why they need to know it. If you relate content to students' personal lives, students have a reason for paying attention to the lesson.

- Whenever the opportunity presents itself, use real-life examples to illustrate a point that you are teaching. Connecting course content to real-life examples motivates students and increases interest.

- Engaging students in real-life projects not only ensures that content will be remembered but enables you to consolidate and teach a large numbers of objectives simultaneously. For example, have students create a Civil War newspaper as a project. Work with students to create a rubric that will be used to assess the newspaper. Each newspaper may include a title, a byline, a table of contents, a feature story with an image, an editorial, an ad, and a crime report. Not only will students demonstrate their comprehension of the Civil War but they will also learn the function of the parts of a newspaper.

- Take students on a field trip to a location that connects the content being taught to the real world. Teachers often wait too late to take the field trip. Taking that trip earlier will make the learning more relevant and provide students with a real-world connection to the content. I still remember taking a field trip to the Young People's Concert, which the Atlanta Symphony sponsored when I was in elementary school. This annual event is one of the reasons that I still possess a love for all different types of music.

- Work-study not only reduces behavioral infractions but also makes content extremely relevant to all brains. For example, when students are placed in alternative education due to their inability to be successful in a regular school setting, they are often involved in work-study or on-the-job training. Career academies and High Schools That Work programs also take advantage of the fact that students learn to do real jobs by doing real jobs. Apprenticeships, internships, practica, and student teaching are all viable and effective ways to help students comprehend and retain knowledge and skill. Assign students to experts in a field who can involve them in a work-study experience related to course content. Then step back and watch them learn!

- Invite guest speakers who are experts in a field of interest to students to come and address the class regarding their profession. Motivating speakers often increase students' knowledge of a particular field of study and may encourage them to pursue the field as a future profession.

REFLECTION

> ### What is my plan for making the learning relevant in my classroom?

Objective/Standard: _____

_____

_____

_____

Connection to Real Life: _____

_____

_____

_____

Objective/Standard: _____

_____

_____

_____

Connection to Real Life: _____

_____

_____

_____

Objective/Standard: _____

_____

_____

_____

Connection to Real Life: _____

_____

_____

_____

Objective/Standard: _____

_____

_____

_____

Connection to Real Life: _____

_____

_____

_____

12

Teach Your Rituals

WHAT: ESTABLISHING YOUR PROCEDURES

I was observing in a classroom in which the teacher had given students specific directions not to disturb her while she was conducting a guided reading group at the back table. Students were also instructed not to talk to their classmates while completing the seatwork that they had been assigned. One student raised his hand and asked, "Mrs. Williams, what are we supposed to do if we have a question about our worksheet?" The teacher replied, "How many times have I told you that if you have a question, ask your neighbor?"

What is wrong with this picture? Was this teacher sending mixed messages? If the class was not supposed to talk, how can this student ask a neighbor if he has a question? As a matter of fact, if the student who raised his hand did ask another student for help, he would now be in trouble for talking.

In every school there are teachers who very effectively manage students. At first it was thought that those teachers had some big bag of tricks that other teachers didn't have that helped them to know just what to do in various situations. What the research is telling us is that effective classroom managers spend an inordinate amount of their time during the first few days and weeks of school establishing their expectations and procedures; in other words, their rituals (Wong & Wong, 1998). They teach all students the specific behaviors expected of them in any classroom situation. These situations include when and how to enter and leave the class, when to talk and how loudly, how to give you their undivided attention when you need it, when and how to distribute papers and how to turn in homework, what to do when absent from school, how to move around the classroom when warranted, and how to return to their seats when the activity is over.

Effective classroom managers anticipate every part of the school day and determine a specific plan to help students successfully navigate through each part. They then teach these rituals to their students in much the same way they teach their content. Students practice, practice, practice until they follow

**"I raised my hand and asked if I could leave
the room, and here I am."**

the rituals habitually and to the satisfaction of the teacher. Effective teachers provide feedback after each practice and celebrate when students get it right. They then spend more time thanking those students who are appropriately practicing the rituals than reprimanding those students who are not.

WHY: THEORETICAL FRAMEWORK

If students are to have equitable opportunities to act appropriately, behavioral expectations must be clearly stated (Davis, 2006).

Students must be taught a teacher's specific academic and behavioral expectations because they vary from one classroom to another (Tileston, 2004).

Teachers should be firm believers in routines and should conscientiously follow them (Crawford, 2004).

Although classrooms should include individualistic, competitive, and cooperative learning activities, the latter enables teachers to teach and students to use the social skills so necessary in the workplace (Tileston, 2004).

Use a stop signal in order to expedite time and manage students in cooperative groups (Crawford, 2004).

Rules need to be written in the affirmative, be brief, and be posted in the classroom (Tileston, 2004).

When students either have been left to their own devices or have not been taught how to act in appropriate ways, their brains are unable to think through the sequence of Emotions (E), Thinking (T), and Action (A) (Divinyi, 2003, p. 4).

Students can be de-stressed through a variety of rituals which give them a feeling of security (Sprenger, 2002).

Many diverse students are not privileged to know the hidden rules of the classroom (Payne, 2001).

Effective teachers use rules as *basic understandings for prosocial behavior before the fact, not after misbehavior has occurred* [emphasis added] (DiGiulio, 2000 p. 22).

The following steps apply when teaching and reviewing classroom procedures:

- Explain the procedure before the activity actually happens.
- Role-play the procedure.
- Practice the procedure and make certain that students understand.
- Provide feedback on the accuracy of the implementation.
- Reteach the procedure as needed.
- Review the procedure prior to implementation every time during the first few weeks of school.
- Review the procedures following holidays (Burden, 2000).

Using routines for entering and leaving the classroom, passing out papers, and participating in cooperative groups provides students with a sense of security (Burden, 2000).

Students should be provided with cues or signals denoting a specific behavior (Burden, 2000).

HOW: CLASSROOM APPLICATION

- Examine every part of each period or of the entire school day and determine what specific procedures students need to learn so that the classroom operates efficiently and effectively. For example, decide what students will do when they enter the room. Will there be a sponge activity on the board? Are students allowed to talk quietly? Once you have determined your procedures or rituals, have students role-play or practice them until they get them correct. Provide feedback after each practice, and celebrate when students perform the rituals to your satisfaction.

- One way to provide specific feedback on your rituals is to tell students, on a scale of 1 to 10, how they are performing. For example, when using chimes to get students' attention, have them role-play talking to a partner and then becoming quiet as soon as they hear the signal. When they get quiet upon hearing the chimes, let them know how well they did. If students rate a 5, then have them continue to practice until they move in the appropriate direction. Celebrate when a 10 is earned!

- If you do a good job of teaching your expectations and procedures, you may need very few rules or even no rules at all. I have visited classrooms where there were so many rules that even the teacher could not keep up with them. Here are a few tips for making decisions regarding the rules you need in your classroom.

  o Limit your rules to three to five maximum.
  o Make sure each rule is stated briefly and in the affirmative, thereby telling students what to do instead of what not to do. For example, the rule *Don't talk unless recognized* should be rephrased to read *Raise your hand when you wish to speak.*
  o Rules should be posted as a constant reminder of your expectations.

- During the first few days of school, have students participate in determining the rituals and rules of your classroom. Students will be more likely to support procedures and rules that they helped create. Teachers have shared with me that the rules that students generate are often stricter than the ones that the teacher intended.

- Save your voice for teaching, and use other things to assist you with management. For example, teach students to look or listen for a signal such as a bell or chime when you need their attention, or raise your hand when you need their attention, and ask them to raise theirs as they end their conversation with a peer. If students do not see your raised hand, they will at least see the hand of a classmate.

- Teach students enough sign language so that you can communicate with them by signing your procedures. For example, when you need students to listen to what you are saying, make the sign for listen and have students sign back to you. When you need them to stop what they are doing, make that sign as well. What a pleasure to have students complying with your requests without saying a word!

- Use energetic music to set time limits on an activity that involves movement or talking. Select a song with a motivational rhythm and play it softly as students complete a task, such as meeting an appointment or reviewing content with a close partner. By the time the song ends, students must have completed their conversations and be ready in case you call on them to respond.

- Use catchy phrases, chants, rhymes, or raps during transition times. Vanessa Anderson, a teacher at Cleveland Elementary School in

Spartanburg, South Carolina, uses the following rap as her fifth- and sixth-grade boys transition from one subject area to another:

One, Two	What should we do?
Three, Four	Listen up once more.
Five, Six	My hands and legs are fixed.
Seven, Eight	I'm sitting up straight.
Nine, Ten	I'm ready for learning again.

By the time the class finishes reciting the rhyme, students have all the necessary materials out and available and are in their seats ready for the next lesson. I observed this ritual working beautifully in her class.

• Rather than wait for students to forget or fail to comply with a procedure and then reprimand them, cue them about the expected behavior prior to the procedure. Cues are reminders of the appropriate behaviors prior to a particular task or event. Cues increase the likelihood that the proper behaviors will be followed and probably need to be used until the expectations and procedures become a habit in students' brains, which takes approximately 21 days.

• When students are having difficulty comprehending your expectations and procedures, a T-chart may be warranted. T-charts delineate exactly what behaviors are expected of students and can be beneficial for teaching social skills as well. For example, often teachers will have a rule that states, "Respect one another." The problem is that different students have different perceptions of the term *respect*. Design a T-chart around the word *respect*. Have students brainstorm ideas as to what respect looks like and sounds like (see the example below). Post the T-chart as a constant reminder of what the specific behaviors are that you expect whenever you ask a student to comply with the rule "Respect one another."

T-Chart

Respect

Looks Like	*Sounds Like*
• One person talking at a time	• "Please"
• Taking turns	• "Thank you"
• Heads nodding in agreement or disagreement	• "I disagree"
• Smiles	• "Excuse me"
• Eye contact	• "Your turn"
• Undivided attention	• Applause

REFLECTION

> **What are the specific rituals/procedures**
> **I need for effectively managing my classroom (such as**
> **when students should talk, when to move, and so forth)?**

Ritual/Procedure: _____

_____

_____

Ritual/Procedure: _____

_____

_____

Ritual/Procedure: _____

_____

_____

Ritual/Procedure: _____

_____

_____

Ritual/Procedure: _____

_____

_____

Ritual/Procedure: _____

_____

_____

Ritual/Procedure: _____

_____

_____

Ritual/Procedure: _____

_____

_____

Ritual/Procedure: _____

_____

_____

> ## What rules do I need, if any, for effective management of my students?

1. _____

_____

_____

_____

2. _____

_____

_____

_____

3. _____

_____

_____

_____

4. _____

_____

_____

_____

5. _____

_____

_____

_____

13

Let Them Talk!

WHAT: CONVERSATION AND THE BRAIN

Since rhymes are brain-compatible, I wrote an original one to symbolize what we teachers and administrators do to students in schools. It is as follows:

Students can't talk in class.

They can't talk in the hall.

They can't talk in the cafeteria.

They can't talk at all!

Did you like my original effort? If the brain is a social organism, then why are student brains not allowed to socialize in class to learn what they need to know? I will never forget my sixth-grade math teacher, Mr. Mitchell, who did not allow us to talk, ever! Even when he was out of the room, he appointed a class monitor who wrote down the names of any student who talked. Anyone whose name appeared on the list was required to stay after school. When he returned to class, if he heard any noise at all or was having a bad day, he kept the entire class after school. What good did it do me to behave if I was going to be kept after school anyway? I made up my mind right then and there that when I became a teacher, I would never keep the entire class after school for what a few students were doing. And, I never did! I now know, however, that talking in class should never have been deemed misbehavior. In fact, one of the best things a student can do is *talk back to you!* Teachers should be asking questions and students supplying answers as much as possible. Unless students respond orally, how will you know that they are with you?

The neuroscientists are telling us that the person in the classroom who is doing the most talking is growing the most dendrites (brain cells). Why is this the case? Let's consider two reasons. First, when a person opens the mouth to speak, that action sends oxygen to the brain, which wakes the brain up and makes it more alert. How alert have you been after sitting in a boring staff development class for a half or full day? Since the brain does not wish to be bored, teachers often bring papers to grade, books to read, or even work to do, so that even in the most boring of circumstances, the brain is at least occupied.

Oxygen is essential to the brain. In fact, if a brain is deprived of oxygen for three to four minutes, one is literally brain dead. I have been in some classrooms, particularly in middle and high school, where students were breathing but it was difficult to tell. They were figuratively brain dead. When the brain is not getting enough oxygen, one yawns, which sends more oxygen to the brain. Note that you seldom yawn when actively engaged in a task, but you yawn a lot more frequently when bored.

In classrooms that are truly brain-compatible, students don't have time to be bored because one of the things that engages their brains is excessive talking. In fact, they should be talking at least twice as much as the teacher. This feat is easier to accomplish than you might expect. An example follows: When you begin a new lesson, often you will be talking to your students, telling them what they need to know. However, when you review the information, you should be asking the questions, and the class should be providing the answers as choral responses. For example, when I teach classes about the physiology of the brain, I ask review questions like the following and have the class provide the answers in a strong, loud, choral response: "How much does the brain weigh?" "Three pounds." "What is the name of the structure over which the two hemispheres talk?" "The corpus callosum." Not only does this activity engage students, but it gives me a pretty good indication of what my class truly remembers of what I just taught them.

When I am pretty sure that students know what they are talking about, I have them talk with a partner, which leads us to the second reason that students should be talking: The brain learns 90% of what it teaches to another brain (Society for Developmental Education, 1995; Sousa, 2001). Teach your students and then have them reteach what you just taught to a partner. You would be surprised how that simple activity enables both partners (teacher and learner) to retain the information.

Many students get in trouble in class for doing the very thing that comes naturally to the brain: talking. Let them talk! Aloud to you, and then to a partner. By the time the information has been bantered about three times, most brains will have it. Use the brains of other students to help you teach content. In my classes, there is the following rule: Ask three, then me! If students have a question about what you are teaching, they should ask three peers prior to asking you.

Teachers often ask me, "What if they talk about something else when they are supposed to be discussing the course content?" This is what I tell them. I give my students permission to talk about whatever they want, provided they have discussed the assignment first and are ready to respond should I call on them. The simple act of telling them that what they have to say is important alleviates a great deal of the sneaking around and off-task behavior that gets so many students in trouble.

WHY: THEORETICAL FRAMEWORK

The quiet classroom where students are raising their hands to speak is not congruent with the way many diverse cultures communicate (Davis, 2006).

Teachers help students strengthen memory when they provide opportunities for them to teach the entire class, partners, or small groups (Tileston, 2004).

Rather than striving for continued focus or complete silence, teachers should build in collaborative or talk time for students (Crawford, 2004).

The amount of time spent on direct instruction with students should be directly tied to the student's age. For example, if the student is six, expect them to attend for six minutes without needing to change to a different activity. From age 15 to adult, 20 minutes is the limit on listening without the benefit of activity (Tileston, 2004).

Because one student's ideas encourage other students to search their neural networks for similar ideas, brainstorming and discussion are good strategies for activating prior knowledge (Gregory & Chapman, 2002).

Students should be provided with opportunities to talk with one another because the brain needs breaks in the learning (Tileston, 2004).

When same-sex companions were separated from their peers and not allowed to talk to them, they showed a dramatic increase in cortisol (the stress hormone) levels from 18% to 87% (Levine, Baukol, & Pavlidis, 1999).

A student's brain is not trained to pay close attention for long periods of time and is better at immediate change (Jensen, 1997).

Social climate strongly influences the way the brain processes information (Cacioppo, Gardner, & Berntson, 1999).

A main component in the success of cooperative learning is its ability to free students from the fear that shuts the brain down and negatively impacts its ability to learn (Dougherty, 1997).

Students learn 90% of the content if they teach it to other students (Society for Developmental Education, 1995).

Positive social context strengthens the immune system (Padgett et al.) while restricting the contact of humans with one another negatively influences the body's reaction to stress (Meany, Sapolsky, & McEwen, 1985).

HOW: CLASSROOM APPLICATION

• When students come into your class, allow them to talk quietly until they begin a sponge activity or until you start the daily lesson. If you have some type of calming music playing (such as classical, jazz, or New Age), you can encourage them to talk beneath the sound of the music. In fact, tell them that if you can hear their individual voices, then they are talking too loudly.

• The brain needs specific feedback if it is to understand exactly what behavior is expected of it. When students talk with one another, give them feedback as to the noise level you expect. You can provide this feedback with comments such as, "Class, you are talking at Level 5; I need you to have Level 3 voices." Let them practice using Level 3 voices until it becomes natural for them. When they accomplish the level you desire, celebrate their success!

• When you need students' attention, you need it at a moment's notice, and you should not have to scream or yell over their talking to get it. After all, *Shouting Won't Grow Dendrites!* Devise a signal for getting students' attention. It can be as simple as a raised hand, the ringing of chimes, or the clapping of hands. It doesn't matter what signal you use as long as you have one. Teach the signal to your students on the first day of school and reinforce it throughout the year. In fact, brains get tired of the same signal all of the time, so vary your attention getters.

• Have each student select a close partner (CP), someone in the class who sits so close to them that they can talk to this person without getting out of their seat. Have students talk to their close partner whenever time is limited and you need students to reteach information just taught, brainstorm ideas, or review pertinent content prior to a test. Close partners can also be used to re-explain something when it is not easily understood.

• Place students in cooperative groups or families of three to five members. Assign these families tasks to complete related to the lesson you are teaching. For example, families can discuss what they know about a given topic or be given specific discussion questions to get them talking. When I taught a model lesson recently in an alternative school, many students were almost asleep or disengaged when I entered the room. However, since the assignment had been to read the book *The Giver,* each student was soon engaged in a discussion of the following question: Is there really such a thing as utopia? You could immediately see the change in student demeanor when they began talking about a subject of interest.

• After you have taught a segment of content, stop and ask questions of the entire class to ascertain whether they have understood and retained the information just taught. Encourage everyone in the class to answer your questions in loud, strong, choral responses. You may even have them stand up in an effort to send more blood and oxygen to the brain while they are answering your designated questions and reviewing content.

• Engage the entire class in brainstorming or discussing ideas related to a selected topic. Brainstorming and discussion not only get students talking, but this strategy also assists students' brains in activating prior knowledge.

• Have students generate their own questions to ask peers regarding course content or a reading selection. Students are more motivated when answering their own queries rather than those provided by the teacher or textbook (Report of the National Reading Panel, 2000).

REFLECTION

> ## What is my plan for incorporating appropriate talk time into my classroom?

What activities will I use that enable students to talk with their peers about content?

_____

_____

_____

_____

_____

_____

_____

What rituals will I use to signal the beginning and ending of talk time for my students (Example: chimes, signals, bells, whistles)?

_____

_____

_____

_____

_____

_____

_____

_____

14

Let Them Move!

WHAT: MOVEMENT AND THE BRAIN

It is 8:55 A.M.—time to change classes in Washington High School. Students are relieved because they get to actually move their bodies to the next location. However, in most middle or high schools, that is probably the last time they will get to move for the next 55 minutes, or until the bell rings for the next period. In fact, if any student attempts to move during the period, that student is in trouble for being out of seat.

If the purpose of the brain is to help the body survive in the real world and in the real world people actually move, then why can't brains achieve that purpose in school? Consider this: There are some things that you know how to do that you will never forget how to do, even if you live to be 100 (e.g., driving a car or riding a bike). You remember these activities because you were moving when you learned them, which meant that the information was placed in one of the strongest memory systems in the brain: procedural or muscle memory. Procedural memory and episodic memory, another memory pathway, are both accessed when students are actively engaged in the learning process. If you have ever taken a computer course, you know that unless you placed your hands on the keyboard during the course and then continued to practice what you learned, your brain did not retain the new skill. Having students do the Number Line Hustle to add positive and negative integers, role-play vocabulary words to retain their meaning, or conduct an experiment to draw conclusions regarding a given hypothesis will go a long way toward ensuring that they will not only retain the concepts being taught but also have fun in the process.

Movement also has a therapeutic effect on the brain and body. This is why people usually feel so much better after they walk or engage in other forms of exercise. Getting students kinesthetically involved in a lesson or walking a student down the hall when he or she is angry tends to calm that student's brain down (Jensen, 2000b; Thayer, 1996).

During a few of my afterschool workshops, I have noticed that some teachers are not in the best frame of mind when they arrive because they have been required to attend. Chances are they have never been in one of my workshops and have expectations of inactivity and boredom. The sooner I get them up and moving, the faster I see the state of their brain change from negative to positive. Why is this? In the brain there are positive and negative chemicals called neurotransmitters. Some of the positive ones are produced when people are moving—chemicals like endorphins, serotonin, and dopamine. These can be very beneficial for students because they not only assist them in remembering content, but they also contribute to the joy of learning.

WHY: THEORETICAL FRAMEWORK

The neural connections in an adolescent's cerebellum are strengthened when that adolescent is involved in bodily-kinesthetic movement, such as physical education classes or extracurricular activities (Feinstein, 2004).

Adolescents are motivated by learning experiences that involve a great deal of time on task, purposeful interactions, and meaningful movement (Crawford, 2004).

Physical activity adds to the amount of oxygen in the blood, which the brain uses as fuel (Sousa, 2001).

Most students, including those in poverty, need many kinesthetic activities because they do not perform well when they have to sit and listen to lectures for very long amounts of time (Tileston, 2004).

A teacher's purposeful use of her classroom space helps to facilitate an adolescent's activity, movement, and learning (Crawford, 2004).

Movement combines mind, body, and emotion, ensuring that learning is meaningful and will be retained (Jensen, 2003).

Even though we know that movement facilitates brain function and a student's ability to learn, high school students spend the majority of their time sitting (Sousa, 2001).

Specific movements enable the brain to release noradrenaline and dopamine, neurotransmitters that assist students in increasing their levels of energy and helping them to feel better (Jensen, 2000b).

While movement increases cognitive function, it also enables students to concentrate better because movement assists students in ridding their bodies of kinesthetic energy (Sousa, 2001).

When students are seen daydreaming, yawning, writing notes, or squirming in their seats, a change of activity is warranted (Burden, 2000).

When movement and other sensory experiences are used with autistic and ADHD students, their ability to pay attention when completing a task or listen when classmates are talking is improved (Sousa, 2001).

Twenty years of research have taught us that movement puts all brains, regardless of age, in the best state for learning (Thayer, 1996).

Movement not only increases learning but creativity, health, and stress management as well (Hannaford, 1995).

Movement is the door to learning (Dennison, 1990).

HOW: CLASSROOM APPLICATION

- As content is discussed, have students stand if they agree with a statement and remain seated if they disagree with it. This simple procedure actively engages both brain and body and can prevent behavior problems.

- When there is something that must be read aloud, have specific groups of students or the entire class stand and read the assigned material aloud. Simply having students stand will wake them up and make them more alert.

- Have students draw a clock with the following four times on it: 12:00, 3:00, 6:00, and 9:00. Have them draw one line near each time. Then they walk around the room to music and make one appointment with each of four different classmates who sit at a distance from them. After students have been sitting for a while, have them stand and move to one of the classmates they made an appointment with to discuss an assigned topic. Just standing and walking will add more blood and oxygen to the brain and facilitate learning.

- Have students make a seasonal appointment with four peers who sit at a distance from them. They will make a summer, fall, winter, and spring appointment with four different students as you assign specific information that needs to be discussed or tasks that need to be completed. When you need to integrate movement into your lesson, have students keep one of their appointments.

- Have students role-play cross-curricular vocabulary or concepts. For example, in a mathematics class, have them use their arms to make obtuse, acute, and right angles. In a language arts class have them act out the definitions of literary terms or reading vocabulary. These terms will be long remembered.

- Body spelling enables students to associate movement with the letters in words. For example, to spell the word *play*, students would bend toward the floor for the *p* and the *y* because those letters drop below the line. Students would spread their arms out to the side for the *a* in *play* because that letter remains on the line, and students would raise their arms toward the sky for the *l* because that letter extends above the line. Once students get the hang of it, they will be body spelling words like photosynthesis or antiestablishment.

- Play games with students to teach or reinforce content. Most games require some type of movement. Competing in a Jeopardy game while standing in teams, tossing a ball as students provide answers while reviewing for a test, or conducting a scavenger hunt to find hidden clues around the school are all examples of games that not only require movement but also produce lots of laughter.

- Involve students in activities that engage the brain in solving real-world problems or completing real-life projects. Designate a number of objectives that can be met through one project, and have students work individually or in teams to complete it. Project- and problem-based instruction pays big dividends toward understanding and retention.

- When students have been working intently for a long period of time, provide them with a stretch break. Have them stand and stretch their bodies to music as they make an effort to relax. This will give their brain a few minutes of much needed down time.

- Consult the text *Worksheets Don't Grow Dendrites: 20 Instructional Strategies That Engage the Brain* for more than 150 ways to actively engage student brains in learning. You will find that the more actively involved students are, the less you will have to deal with the major causes of misbehavior: boredom, attention, control, and inadequacy.

REFLECTION

What is my plan for incorporating movement into my lessons?

What activities will I use that enable students to move as they are learning?

Objective/Standard: _____

Activity to Incorporate Movement: _____

_____

_____

Objective/Standard: _____

Activity to Incorporate Movement: _____

_____

_____

Objective/Standard: _____

Activity to Incorporate Movement: _____

_____

_____

Objective/Standard: _____

Activity to Incorporate Movement: _____

_____

_____

Objective/Standard: _____

Activity to Incorporate Movement: _____

_____

_____

What rituals will I use to signal the beginning and end of movement for my students?

_____

_____

_____

_____

15

Accentuate the Positive

WHAT: CREATING AN AFFIRMING CLASSROOM ENVIRONMENT

If your students like you, there is nothing they won't do *for* you!

If your students don't like you, there is nothing they won't do *to* you.

I am a trainer for *The 7 Habits of Highly Effective People.* During that workshop a concept is taught called the *Emotional Bank Account.* The *Emotional Bank Account* is a metaphor for the relationships that we establish with one another. We make deposits (positive interactions) and withdrawals (negative interactions) in other people's emotional bank accounts. However, just as in the case of financial accounts, if you make larger or more frequent withdrawals than you make deposits, you are soon overdrawn or even bankrupt with that person.

Let's apply this concept to the classroom. Many teachers have overdrawn or bankrupt relationships with their students because they spend the majority of their time trying to think of all the consequences or punishments (withdrawals) that can be administered to stop unacceptable behavior. This puts the teacher and student on the negative side of their emotional bank accounts. Now change the paradigm. Let's find more ways to positively affirm the good things that students do (deposits) so that when we have to make a withdrawal we have at least built up a positive account with the student. In fact, solid relationships are built when, for every withdrawal, there are eight to ten deposits. In other words, for every time in class I have to reprimand a student or give a consequence for misbehavior, there should be many times that I have complimented the same student for good or improved behavior and acceptable class work. If you look for the good in students, you can find it!

The deposits many teachers use involve extrinsic rewards. There is evidence from the field of economics that they do have their place (Lazear, 2000). Stickers, stars, privileges, and so on appear to provide positive reinforcement for the desired behaviors. In fact, extrinsic rewards tend to be more effective when they are tied to the student's specific performance and not to the student him- or herself.

The field of psychology, however, lends a word of caution to this scenario. Rewards can inhibit performance and appear to become negative reinforcers in the long term (Deci, Koestner, & Ryan, 1999). Affirmations, celebrations, choice, feedback, and peer interactions can be more effective for the increased long-term motivation of your students.

"Your heart is slightly bigger than the average human heart, but that's because you're a teacher."

WHY: THEORETICAL FRAMEWORK

Effective teachers strive to catch students being good and make certain that their parents know about it as well (Orange, 2005).

When students are asked what they feel, what they think, and what they know regarding a given situation, they will often give honest answers (Smith, 2004).

The brain does not do its best work when a system of reward and punishment is used (Tileston, 2004).

When students feel positively connected to their teacher, they are more likely to become a part of the class and less likely to misbehave (Smith, 2004).

Since the brain prefers positive phrases to negative ones, it is better to use short phrases that tell a student to do the right thing than to use negative phrases to tell them what not to do (Divinyi, 2003).

Before we can expect students to focus on the curriculum, they must feel physically and psychologically safe (Sousa, 2001).

Many students have to establish a relationship with their teachers before they can learn from them (Haycock, 2001; Payne, 2001).

Stickers, coupons, awards, and other *symbolic tokens of recognition* do not dampen the intrinsic motivation of students if the tokens are awarded when the student accomplishes very specific performance goals (Marzano, Pickering, & Pollok, 2001).

Rewards can often be very effective but have the following drawbacks: (1) the student comes to expect the reward; (2) the student may decide that the reward is no longer important; and (3) a system of reward is difficult to maintain because rewards need to be immediate and intermittent (Koenig, 2000).

It is better to praise what the student did rather than the student personally so that the teacher can encourage the student to accomplish the achievement again (Wong & Wong, 1998).

In most classrooms, 99% of the positive feedback goes to the positive, well-disciplined students. The ones who are misbehaving need it just as much, if not more (Koenig, 2000).

When learners have some choice or control over their learning environment, motivation is increased. Therefore, teachers should design learning experiences that enable students to meet their own personal academic, health, social, and career goals (Jensen, 1995).

Effective teachers are warm, caring, and lovable people who invite students to engage in learning (Wong & Wong, 1998).

Consider the following positive alternatives to rewards: support from peers, rituals, enthusiasm, more feedback, increased options for creativity, self-assessment, and more student choice and control (Jensen, 1995).

> When the brain is experiencing stress from a system of rewards, it is unable to do higher-level thinking or change its perceptual maps (Jensen, 1995).
>
> When students earn a reward for attaining a goal, the neurotransmitter dopamine is released, which trains their brains to have positive feelings about the reward rather than the goal attainment (Kohn, 1993).
>
> Anxiety exists when students' challenges are greater than their skills. Boredom exists when a student's skills are greater than the challenges. When skill level and challenge align, you have flow or the perfect state for learning (Csikszentmihalyi & Csikszentmihalyi, 1990).
>
> Rewards do not work if the objective is any of the following: sustaining quality student performance; producing learners who are self-directed; fostering creative students who use higher-order thinking skills; producing honest, self-confident, highly-motivated students (Kohn, 1993).
>
> A 20-year study by a Brandeis University researcher resulted in the finding that over the long haul, rewards just do not work. Creativity in artists declined when they had previously signed a contract selling the work when it was completed (Amabile, 1989).

HOW: CLASSROOM APPLICATION

- Be certain that your classroom exudes a positive learning environment—one that is both physically and psychologically safe. A positive environment includes smiles, friendly greetings, students' support for one another, celebrations—and the absence of sarcasm or threats, which shut the brain down to learning or higher-level thinking. Your room may be the one bright spot in a student's otherwise dismal day.

- Get acquainted with each student personally and call them by name daily. That is much more difficult to do at the middle and high school level when you have multiple classes; however, it is still essential to building a positive environment. Stand at the door each morning or period and warmly greet students each day. Take a personal interest in students. If you know that one played on the football team during the weekend, ask him whether he won the game. If a student has a new hairdo, positively comment on the change. You would be surprised what a positive difference these simple comments can make to your relationship with a student!

- Teach your students to follow your rituals for effective classroom management. If you must have some rules, make sure they number no more than three to five. Be certain that they are stated positively so that they tell students what to do rather than what not to do. For example, when you yell to a student who is speeding down the hall, "Don't run!" his or her brain hears the word *run* the loudest. It is better to tell the student, "Walk!"

- Use rewards such as stickers, stars, and coupons sparingly. Whenever they are used, be certain that they are tied to students' specific performance and not to the student personally.

- Some students who are consistently having trouble following your procedures may need individual behavior charts. The chart should list no more than one or two behaviors you will be observing for each individual student. Whenever you see the student exhibiting those behaviors, a check mark can be made on the card. When the student has a designated number of daily checks, the student is entitled to some type of predetermined reward.

- Provide students with choice whenever possible as a positive alternative to rewards. For example, allow students to engage in a variety of instructional strategies when delivering content (see Table I in the Introduction), or give them several ways to demonstrate what they have learned on an assessment. Allow them to select who they will make appointments with to discuss class content. When students have choice, they feel some measure of control over their environment.

- Notify parents via telephone or pager when their children have done something exceptional. This simple technique will have two-fold results. You will be indirectly making a deposit in the student's bank account while the parents will be so surprised at a positive contact from you that they will be simultaneously making a deposit to their child's account as well.

- Since the brain loves celebration, celebrate even minor, but deserved, successes in the classroom. Let students know that you appreciate their improved efforts by incorporating the 25 celebrations outlined in Chapter 16 of this book.

- Play music with motivating lyrics and an enthusiastic beat to create a positive environment. Examples of songs are included in Chapter 5.

- Provide students with specific reasons for praise. If you walk around the classroom consistently saying Very good! Great! Excellent! Great job! day after day, students will be very tired of the rhetoric in a very short amount of time. However, if you find specific reasons to congratulate students for a job well done, the effect is much greater. For example, tell Julie that the opening paragraph of her paper used so many descriptive adjectives that it grabbed the reader's attention from the very beginning. Tell Marvin that you noticed that he was able to stay in his seat for a longer period today and that you really appreciate the effort.

- There appear to be three major types of positive reinforcers: tangible reinforcers, social reinforcers, and privileges.
  - Tangible reinforcers include candy, stickers, treats, and other types of rewards given for specific positive behaviors displayed. This is the least desirable type of reinforcer, and its use often leads to the student asking, "If I complete this assignment, what do I get?"
  - Privileges include extra computer or recess time, being appointed line leader or student of the day, or being given no

homework passes. These are better than tangibles as positive reinforcers but are still not the best.

o   The final type is the social reinforcer. These include verbal praise, hugs, handshakes and other forms of celebration, positive notes or phone calls home to parents, and written comments to the student. This is the preferred type to use because in the real world adults receive social reinforcers most often. For example, I don't think I have ever gotten a sticker for cooking a good dinner, but I have received a compliment from my husband or children for a delicious meal. If your students are always looking for tangibles or privileges then, at the very least, pair the tangible with a social reinforcer. In other words, tell the students why they are receiving the candy or no homework passes. Then gradually reduce the number of tangibles or privileges given, but keep the social reinforcers coming. They're good for the brain!

REFLECTION

What are 10 things I can do to create a positive learning environment in my classroom?

1. _____

2. _____

3. _____

4. _____

5. _____

6. _____

7. _____

8. _____

9. _____

10. _____

16

Celebrate Good Times, Come On!

WHAT: CELEBRATIONS AND THE BRAIN

At the end of the course *Worksheets Don't Grow Dendrites*, which I teach to administrators and teachers all over the world, we celebrate the vast amount of information that we have learned. Participants learn more from me in one day than they learn in some workshops in one week. We move eight steps to the left and right to the song *Celebration* by Kool and the Gang. This culminating activity practically ensures that participants will leave the workshop with a feeling of euphoria and jubilance.

The brain loves celebrations. No matter how small the improvement, students and their teacher should show their appreciation for increases in student learning or behavior by a preponderance of celebrations. This chapter will provide 25 ways that students and teachers can create a positive climate through celebrations and affirmations.

In more classrooms than I care to count, I have observed students who make a habit of pointing out the imperfections in the personalities, looks, and abilities of their classmates. They make sarcastic remarks, demean, and deride one another—sometimes to get attention, sometimes to feel more in control, and sometimes just to be mean.

In a brain-compatible classroom where threats are diminished and confidence increased, no place exists for this negative type of behavior. Threats place the brain in survival mode and make it difficult, if not nearly impossible, to learn at optimal levels. This is why in Maslow's hierarchy, survival and psychological needs are placed below academic pursuits (Boeree, 1998). Survival needs must be satisfied before academic needs are even taken into consideration.

When a teacher affirms a student's correct answer or when students celebrate the accomplishments of a peer, a cooperative group, or the class as a whole, confidence increases and the classroom becomes a place where behavior problems are diminished and learning accelerated.

WHY: THEORETICAL FRAMEWORK

Celebrations cause students to laugh. Humor helps students to make a personal connection with the teacher (Chapman & King, 2003).

Celebrations must be relevant and believable and last long enough to tell the brain to release positive chemicals, like dopamine, in the brain (Jensen, 2003).

The more positive acknowledgments the student gets, the better; however, teachers should praise the student's specific accomplishments rather than the student himself or herself (Divinyi, 2003).

Students' brains have to be in a receptive state for celebration if dopamine levels in the brain are to be effectively raised (Jensen, 2003).

A classroom should be a positive place where students feel that "the teacher wants to help them be right rather than catch them being wrong" (Sousa, 2001, p. 44).

Be certain that an affirmation or celebration is deserved. Students must feel that their performance warrants the celebration (Jensen, 2003).

Positive feedback just may be the single most powerful influence on the brain's chemistry and an essential element in helping people develop a healthy self-concept (Sylwester, 1997).

Memory and performance are directly correlated to a positive experience (Pert, 1997).

Just a few moments of laughter can be good for the body and the mind (Dhyan, 1995).

HOW: CLASSROOM APPLICATION

- *High Five.* The high five has always symbolized agreement or acceptance. To high five, raise the open palm of your dominant hand and slap the raised open palm of the dominant hand of a student when that student does something well. Have students high five their learning partner or other students in their cooperative group when the group successfully completes an assignment.

- *Thumbs Up.* Give students a thumbs up to indicate agreement or acknowledgment of a job well done. To form a thumbs up, make a fist with your dominant hand while pointing the thumb of that hand toward the ceiling. Students can give thumbs ups to one another when they agree with a peer's answer.

- *Handshake.* Extend your dominant hand and shake the hand of a student when that student does something noteworthy. Students can give one another handshakes to show their appreciation for a job well done.

- *Pat on the Back.* Tell students to take their dominant hand, reach across their bodies, and pat themselves on the back when they give a correct answer or behave appropriately.

- *Fantastic! Fantastic!* Tell students that their performance is fantastic by pretending that you are pressing the spray on a bottle of *Fantastic.* Make the appropriate noises for a spray bottle as you are pretending to press the spray three times. Then, with the same hand, pretend you are wiping two times while you say the words "Fantastic! Fantastic!" with expression. Students can also spray one another.

- *Great! Great! Great!* To tell students that their performance is Great! Great! Great!, spread your dominant hand out to represent the grater. Your other hand forms a fist to become the ball of cheese. Then pretend to be grating the cheese while you say, "Great! Great! Great!"

- *WOW!* Make a "W" by sticking up only the three middle fingers of your right hand. Place those three fingers to the right side of your mouth. Then form your mouth into a large "O." Finally, stick the three middle fingers of your left hand beside the left side of your mouth. Say the word "WOW" as you make the same word with your fingers and mouth. Students can give one another a "WOW" when the performance is deserved.

- *COOL!* The word "COOL" is made with the fingers and eyes. Take your right hand and make the letter "C" with your thumb and forefinger. Place that "C" beside your right eye. Stretch your eyes wide to make the two "Os" in the word COOL. The "L" is made by turning the palm of the left hand toward you, making the letter "L" with your thumb and forefinger, and turning the other three fingers down. Place the letter "L" next to your left eye so that your fingers and eyes form the word "COOL." Say the word "COOL" with expression as you form the word.

- *Looking Good!* Take the forefinger of your right hand and make the four sides of an imaginary mirror. Make sure you make the sounds as you are forming the sides. Then, once your mirror is made, primp in it by turning your head to the right side and patting the back of it while you say emphatically, "Looking good! Looking good!"

- *Round of Applause.* Have students softly clap their hands together, but as they clap them, have them move their hands around in a large circle so that they literally have a "round of applause."

- *Good Job, Good Buddy!* Pretend that you are a driver in an 18-wheeler. Pretend that you are pulling the cord with your dominant hand, and make the sound a truck makes when it is blowing its horn. Then say, "Good job, good buddy!"

- *Kiss Your Brain!* Tell a student who has given a good answer to "Kiss your brain." The student should then take the dominant hand and place it on the lips and then to the top of the head.

- *Golf Clap.* Pretend you are at a golf game. Gently pat your hands together as if you are applauding the performance of a golfer who has just made a hole in one. You must look prim and proper as you gently clap your hands together. Students can give one another golf claps.

- *Spider Clap.* Have students spread their fingers apart on both hands and then clap the fingers on their right hand together with the corresponding finger on the left hand so that the fingers resemble a spider.

- *Finger Clap.* Have students take the forefingers of the left and right hands and gently clap them together. There should be no sound made at all.

- *Silent Cheer.* Have students hold up both left and right hands beside their head and cheer as enthusiastically as possible; however, no sound at all should come from the lips.

- *Firecracker.* Have students place their hands together and move them into the air much as a firecracker would. They should also make the sounds of a firecracker going into the air. Then they should clap their hands once, separate them, and bring them down slowly while making the sounds of a firecracker's sparks descending.

- *Bravo! Bravo!* Have students stand, clap their hands and shout, "Bravo! Bravo!" just as an audience would do following an outstanding concert or performance. This celebration should be reserved for exceptional performances.

- *Standing O.* Have students give one another Standing Os by standing on their tiptoes and forming an "O" with their arms raised above their heads. This cheer is reserved for truly exceptional answers or performances.

- *Outstanding.* To tell a specific student that his or her performance is outstanding, have each student make a baseball umpire's signal for an "out" and then stand up. This cheer is reserved for the highest quality of answers.

- *Clappers.* Purchase plastic hand clappers from a novelty store. Whenever students give a correct answer or behave appropriately, give them a hand with the plastic clappers. They will feel so good about themselves! These clappers can also be purchased from the Oriental Trading Company catalog.

- *Bell Ringer.* Purchase a small bell and ring it only when students' answers show great insight or their performances demonstrate great creative effort.

- *Light Up!* Buy a rubber light bulb. You may purchase one from Spencer Kagan's catalog. When students are obviously thinking, show them that you appreciate their efforts by passing them the light bulb to hold temporarily. Holding the light bulb is indicative of the "light coming on" in the students' brains.

• *Original Cheers.* When students are working in cooperative groups, or *families,* encourage them to create original cheers that do not last more than a few seconds. Groups can perform these cheers for the class and use them whenever a member of a family, or the family as a whole, does something exceptional. Often the entire class's performance will be noteworthy. Then all *families* can perform their cheers simultaneously.

• *Celebration Music.* Select exuberant songs that will motivate students and help them celebrate their successes, for example, *We Are the Champions* by Queen; *Celebration* by Kool and the Gang; *I Got the Power* by Snap; *Gonna Fly Now!,* the theme from *Rocky; New Attitude* by Patti LaBelle; or *I Just Want to Celebrate* by Rare Earth.

REFLECTION

> ## Which celebrations will I use
> ## in my classroom to affirm my students and
> ## commemorate successful performances?

1. _____
   _____
   _____
   _____

2. _____
   _____
   _____
   _____

3. _____
   _____
   _____
   _____

4. _____
   _____
   _____
   _____

5. _____
   _____
   _____
   _____

17

Use Low-Profile Interventions

WHAT: INTERVENING APPROPRIATELY

I was observing in a classroom a few years ago when I noticed the following scenario. A history teacher was lecturing from the front of the room when she noticed that a student was paying little attention to the lecture. Instead, the student appeared to be intently interested in a page in his history book. However, the teacher also noticed that there was something sticking out of the history book. Upon practicing proximity and moving closer to the student, the teacher observed a comic book inserted in the history text. Prior to this time, I was the only one who knew that this was going on, and I only knew because the student's desk was directly in front of where I was seated in the rear of the room.

The angry teacher felt compelled to point out the disciplinary infraction to the entire class. She indicated to the class how disgusted she was with the student and requested sarcastically that he read a few pages from the comic book aloud to the entire class. The student responded with a "smart aleck" remark. Soon both teacher and student were involved in a shouting match that ended when the teacher ordered the student out of her classroom.

This entire incident could have been avoided if the teacher had used a *low-profile intervention.* Low-profile interventions are techniques that proactive teachers use that are likely to correct misbehavior without negatively impacting the teacher's ability to deliver instruction. A low-profile intervention, in the above scenario, would have been to move closer to the student and tap the desk lightly, indicating to the student that the comic book should be put away—all the while continuing to teach. In this way, the behavioral infraction may have been resolved without the entire class being aware of what was happening and having to endure the disruptive effects of a power struggle.

Other low-profile interventions include the following: eye contact, signaling, pausing, ignoring, proximity, and touching.

WHY: THEORETICAL FRAMEWORK

Eye contact from the teacher seems to quiet students down immediately because when students are making eye contact with the teacher, they find it difficult to talk at the same time (Smith, 2004).

Telling students that a request is a *Nike Issue* means that they should *Just Do It* without arguing or negotiating, even if they don't want to do it (Divinyi, 2003, p. 77).

Teachers should speak in a clear, direct, and firm yet soft voice when addressing the class (Smith, 2004).

Signaling, reminding, warning, praising, and ignoring are all forms of "low-key discipline" (Kottler, 2002).

The following nonverbal and nonpunitive responses may be used to get students back on task:

- ignoring;
- nonverbal signals;
- proximity or standing near a student;
- supportive touching (Burden, 2000).

Proximity, or moving near students while teaching, helps to keep their attention focused (Smith, 2004).

The following low-profile interventions can be effective in redirecting students back to the task:

- Use the student's name in a lesson.
- Use humor, not sarcasm, directed at the situation or yourself.
- Send an *I-message* to remind students that their behavior affects other students.
- Use positive phrasing by stating the way in which appropriate behavior can lead to positive outcomes.
- Remind students of the rules.
- Provide students with choices (Burden, 2000).

HOW: CLASSROOM APPLICATION

- When certain forms of misbehavior become apparent, move closer to the offending student in the hope that your proximity will eradicate the infraction. For example, if two students are talking at the back of the room while you are teaching at the front, practice proximity and move closer to the students without making mention of their conversation.

- Some teachers are masters of the low-profile intervention of eye contact. Simply looking at students without saying a word can be very effective, especially if they know that you mean business.

• If the primary goal of a student's misbehavior is to get attention, sometimes simply ignoring the behavior is the most appropriate response. Behaviors that could eventually cause harm to other students should never be ignored.

• Reminding students of the specific procedures that are required (cueing) prior to the implementation of an activity helps to ensure that students comply with established rituals. See Chapter 12 for additional information regarding the process of cueing.

• A hand on a student's shoulder can be a low-profile intervention that provides a calming touch to a misbehaving student. Make sure the touch is truly calming and not antagonistic.

• Incorporating the student's name in an example may refocus his or her attention. Be sure that the name is not used in a derogatory way. An example would be the following: David is off-task. The teacher says, "I know that David likes to draw, and we could use his expertise in critiquing this next painting."

• When you use a ritual to get students' attention, such as ringing chimes or raising your hand, and students do not get quiet immediately, simply pause until you get what you want. If you talk over their talking you send the message that what you have to say to students is not nearly as important as what students have to say to one another.

• Use *I-messages* when addressing misbehavior, such as, "I was disappointed when you failed to show up for class on time," or "I can never allow students in this class to ridicule one another since we are a family and work together." Putting the emphasis on you rather than the student de-escalates the situation.

• If rules or procedures are posted on your wall, simply pointing to a rule without speaking can remind students that they may not be complying with it.

• When students are becoming upset and raise their voices when talking to you or a classmate, most teachers have a tendency to raise their voices as well. Do the opposite. When students raise their voices, lower yours. It will calm, rather than escalate, the situation. Remember, *Shouting Won't Grow Dendrites.*

REFLECTION

**What are some low-profile interventions
that I can use to correct misbehavior
while continuing to teach?**

1. _____

   _____

2. _____

   _____

3. _____

   _____

4. _____

   _____

5. _____

   _____

6. _____

   _____

7. _____

   _____

8. _____

   _____

9. _____

   _____

10. _____

   _____

18

Deemphasize the Negative

WHAT: CONSEQUENCES FOR MISBEHAVIOR

When I teach my *Worksheets Don't Grow Dendrites* course, I engage participants in an unforgettable activity in which they pair up and become Partners A and B. Partner A asks Partner B to extend his or her dominant arm out to the side. While the arm is extended, Partner A pushes down on the arm and asks Partner B to resist and at the same time think of something positive in his or her life, something that makes him or her feel good, or something that makes him or her smile. The arm typically stays strong and cannot be pulled down no matter the pressure. Partner A then asks Partner B to think of a time when he or she was upset, angry, or stressed and repeats the procedure. The arm invariably goes down and everyone is amazed. The procedure is then repeated with the roles reversed.

The purpose of this activity is to convince people of the body's reaction when the brain is thinking both positively and negative. For example, when the brain is thinking positively, the arm stays raised due to the body's ability to appropriately perform when the brain has confidence and is thinking good thoughts. This is the reason that a baseball player will often get a hit and then come back later in the game and get another hit. After all, success breeds success! When the brain is thinking negatively, the arm is pushed down easily due to the fact that anger, stress, and fear are a threat to the brain. When the brain is threatened, it prepares the body to defend itself against the threat by sending blood to the extremities. Blood flow is reduced in the brain, one is not able to think at higher levels, and the body does not perform appropriately. This is why a baseball player who makes one error will often make another one. This is also the reason that a stressed or angry teacher is not capable of making the best decisions regarding effective consequences for students. When both teacher and student are affected, power struggles ensue and no one truly wins. Even if the teacher orders the student out of the room, the student has received the attention or power that he or she desired all along.

There appear to be three reasons that teachers continue using ineffective discipline methods: (1) Behaviors are deeply embedded when they are learned through imitation and observation; (2) Habits are difficult to break; and (3) When ineffective methods work part of the time, teachers believe that if they are persistent, the methods will work again (Koenig, 2000).

Proactive classroom managers create a positive classroom environment in which confidence is encouraged and threat discouraged, where students feel both physically and psychologically safe. They know that while consequences may stop misbehavior in the short term, it is the positive interactions that change behavior in the long run. When disruptions do occur, these teachers first try a low-profile intervention, as described in the previous chapter. If they have to resort to a high-profile intervention or implement a consequence, they do so in a calm manner, demonstrating

"Wow! I had no idea aspirin came in such large bottles."

SOURCE: Copyright © 2003, Aaron Bacall, *The Lighter Side of Teaching*. Thousand Oaks, CA: Corwin Press.

the respect for the student that they also expect for themselves. They send the message to the student that they care about him or her but will not tolerate the inappropriate behavior that the student has chosen.

A consequence is defined as something that a student would not want to happen but is not physically or psychologically harmful to the student. Consequences are more effective than punishment because in the real world there are both positive and negative consequences for the decisions that people make, and people are usually aware of those consequences prior to making a decision. This chapter will list some possible consequences that may work. I say "may" because each student is different. What works for one may or may not work for another. In fact, many students have experienced such severe consequences, either at home (such as verbal or physical abuse) or at school (such as suspension or expulsion), that one more consequence in a long list will probably make little difference.

While this chapter will examine what the research says about consequences for misbehavior, keep in mind that there are teachers who are so skilled that they do not use consequences at all. Instead, they spend their time equipping students with the skills necessary to exhibit the appropriate behavior in all circumstances.

WHY: THEORETICAL FRAMEWORK

Angry, proactive teachers note their anger and calmly state what the student needs to do. Reactive teachers make the choice to take their anger out on students (Smith, 2004).

The old model of *my way or the highway* is ineffective for today's students and results in a major waste of human life and resources (Tileston, 2004, p. 2).

Natural or logical consequences, those attached to student behavior, enable students to see the connections between the choices they make and the consequences (Smith, 2004).

When students exhibit anger, fear, or power, teachers shouldn't lose their temper, make threats they can't carry out, put students' names on the board, humiliate students, ignore their poor behavior, or treat one student differently from another (Tileston, 2004).

When students either have been left to their own devices or have not been taught how to act in appropriate ways, their brains are unable to think through the sequence of Emotions (E), Thinking (T), and Action (A) (Divinyi, 2003, p. 4).

When a student's behavior goes beyond what you are capable of handling, plan a code for help in advance with another teacher (Tileston, 2004).

Punishment by itself does not assist students' brains in developing the Emotions (E), Thinking (T), and Action (A) sequence (Divinyi, 2003).

Teachers cannot make the assumption that reprimanding or punishing students when they act inappropriately will result in behavior change (Tileston, 2004).

One way to keep from getting into a verbal power struggle with a student is to practice the *Two Sentence Rule,* which means telling the student what is expected in two sentences only and then stopping (Divinyi, 2003, p. 90).

Lecturing is usually ineffective in preventing behavior problems because it may either cause a student to feel embarrassed and retaliate or it may leave the impression that if caught, there is not a more severe consequence than being yelled at or lectured (Koenig, 2000).

Complaining in the teacher's lounge about how terrible your students are may win you sympathy temporarily but is counterproductive and only reinforces the false assumption that students are purposely setting out to make your life miserable (Kottler, 2002).

Threatening students may be ineffective because angry threats cause angry responses, escalate power struggles that erode cooperation, and are laden with empty promises that students know will never be carried out (Koenig, 2000).

While the whole point of punishment is to change behavior, it often does not (Divinyi, 2003).

Responding to an angry, loud student with a loud voice only escalates the student's anger (Koenig, 2000).

Violent or aggressive behavior in students can be escalated with screaming, humiliation, and sarcasm. Teachers should model the calm behavior that they expect others to exhibit (Kottler, 2002).

While providing consequences for misbehavior can be very effective, punishment has some definite disadvantages. It may cause some students to seek revenge. Other students could care less about the punishment. Still others can convince a teacher not to enforce the consequences, leading students to draw the conclusion that they can talk their way out of being punished (Koenig, 2000).

The best consequences are reasonable and logical. Reasonable consequences logically follow from the behavior and are not arbitrary, while logical consequences assist students in choosing between behavior that is acceptable and unacceptable (Wong & Wong, 1998).

HOW: CLASSROOM APPLICATION

• Proactive classroom managers believe in their ability to maintain a well-run classroom and assist students in their ability to manage themselves. Therefore, they are not overheard making any of the following comments: *This is the worse class I have ever had! I don't know what to do with Don! What can you expect when you're teaching these kids?* A well-managed classroom begins with the teacher's belief and visualization that the year will be a great one!

- Be certain that students are fully apprised of your classroom management plan with its rituals or rules, celebrations or rewards, and consequences. Give students a written copy of your plan for students to share with their parents. You may want to have parents sign the plan to ensure that they have reviewed it. Role-play the behaviors you want from students and practice the rituals and provide feedback until students' performance is satisfactory. Once students know your expectations, then it is their choice to comply or not. Having students assist in formulating your management plan for the class helps them take more ownership of it.

- When dealing with an angry student, if the student raises his or her voice, lower yours.

- Conduct a private conference with the student to address the misbehavior.

- When talking with the student, calmly use *I-messages*, which put more of the emphasis on you and not the student. An example of an *I-message* would be as follows: I was disappointed when you chose to disrupt the class. *I-messages* are not as effective when students are extremely angry.

- The most appropriate negative consequences proceed naturally from the misbehavior. For example, a student who purposely knocks over her milk should be asked to clean it up, or a student who makes a mean comment to another should apologize for the insult.

- Deprive the student of a classroom privilege (such as free time or a desirable activity). Prior to the disciplinary infraction, be certain the student knows that loss of a privilege is a possible consequence so you can make it clear that to engage in the misbehavior is a choice the student has made.

- Ask a student who is misbehaving to remove him- or herself from the other students and place him or her in a location in the room known as *time out*. The student goes to time out without work or anything else to do; however, provide the student with an opportunity to rejoin the rest of the class when he or she is willing to be cooperative. When asking the student to move to the time out area, simply state the request politely. If the student does not move, request again. If that does not work, do not force the student to go. Simply say, "I understand that you do not choose to go to time out. We will discuss this later." Then continue teaching.

- If misbehavior persists, contact parents and inform them of the disciplinary infraction. Be sure to convey that you have the best interest of their child at heart and are desirous of working with them to ensure academic achievement. Work with the parents to formulate a plan for the discontinuance of the misbehavior. It is crucially important that the first time you contact a parent the interaction should be a positive one. Either prior to school starting or as soon as possible after the school year begins, contact the parent by phone or in writing and tell him or her how pleased you are to be working with his or her child. Tell him or her that you are expecting to have a great year and are primarily concerned with the success of the child. If the first contact is positive, the parent will be more supportive when contacted for a negative reason.

• While writing should never be used as punishment, having older students create written reflections regarding their misbehavior appears to work in some cases. Students in the intermediate grades or in middle or high school can be required to engage in a reflective writing activity in which they describe the circumstances surrounding the occurrence of the misbehavior, state exactly what the misbehavior was, and state what specific behaviors they can engage in that would lead to a better outcome in the future.

• Students could be removed from the classroom and sent to in-school suspension, a designated room in the school where students are held for a number of hours or days. Students should be provided with academic work and not allowed to talk with other students. Lunch is brought to the student, who works in a confined space. Be certain that being in in-school suspension is undesirable. If it becomes a place where students can be removed from a class that they didn't like in the first place and allowed to socialize with their friends, then it is more of a reward than a consequence.

• Students who persist in misbehavior can be excluded from the class and sent to another room. To employ this consequence, simply arrange ahead of time to pair with a fellow teacher at a very different grade level. You take their students and they take yours. Students are sent for a designated period of time with academic work. The students in the receiving class are told ahead of time to ignore the arriving student. The misbehaving students are told they have chosen not to comply with the rules of this class and are therefore being sent to another room. This consequence should be used very sparingly but can be very effective since a sixth grader, for example, would not want to be seen in a third-grade classroom.

REFLECTION

> **What consequences do I believe
> will be effective in my classroom? (Remember
> that consequences may be necessary but
> should be limited because they tend not to
> change behavior in the long run.)**

Consequence: _____

_____

_____

_____

Consequence: _____

_____

_____

_____

Consequence: _____

_____

_____

_____

Consequence: _____

_____

_____

_____

Consequence: _____

_____

_____

_____

Consequence: _____

_____

_____

_____

19

Get Help With Chronic Behavior Challenges

WHAT: MANAGING THE HARD TO MANAGE

My son, Chris, loved school when he was in the lower grades. He made A's and B's on his report card each semester. In the fourth or fifth grade his love for school began to diminish. This continued through middle school and into high school. Eventually, his grades also diminished proportionately. At first, we thought the decline was due to a lack of motivation and that he just wasn't trying. Therefore, we decided to withhold privileges from him until he improved his grades. However, that just did not happen. Everything had been taken away from him other than the air he breathed, and we observed no change in his academic performance. Chris was not a major behavior problem, but he was having difficulty staying in his seat and concentrating on the task at hand.

In desperation, we had a more in-depth diagnosis made and the doctor surmised that Chris was exhibiting all of the characteristics of attention deficit disorder (ADD). The doctor suggested that he could have a shortage of dopamine in the frontal lobe of the brain. Dopamine is a chemical that assists the brain in focusing and attending to the task at hand. When you consider that one way the brain produces dopamine is through the body's movement, is it any wonder that ADD students move around, even when they're not supposed to?

Since Chris's classes did not afford him the opportunity to experience the very thing his brain needed most, movement, we placed him in a different school where he could be involved in active engagement strategies—project-based instruction, service learning, drawing, the use of manipulatives, field trips called knowledge treks, and so on. Chris's report card in the first reporting period at his new school yielded five A's and one B. We had not seen A's and B's since the primary grades.

You have to understand that while my son experienced challenges in school, he, like other students (especially males), has several gifts. He draws beautifully, can assemble anything with his hands (without looking at the directions), and is a whiz on the computer. There are plenty of job opportunities for Christopher. However, unless his teachers use the 20 instructional strategies delineated in the Introduction of this book, Chris does not experience success in school.

Chris is not alone. I cannot count the many parents I have spoken with whose children exhibit some of the same characteristics as my son. ADD is but one of the chronic challenges with which teachers have to deal. This chapter will describe five of a teacher's major behavior challenges and make some research-based generalizations for meeting the needs of these students as well.

It is important to note that while the chapter delineates several symptoms of each chronic disorder, few students exhibit characteristics of just one. In fact, the term *comorbidity* (overlapping conditions) is used to describe the fact that your greatest behavior challenges reflect symptoms from several different disorders, making it difficult to discern exactly which disorder takes precedence. Therefore, the majority of classroom application activities in this chapter will apply regardless of the specific disorder. Eric Jensen's text, *Different Learners, Different Brains: How to Reach the Hard to Teach* (2000a), is an exceptional resource for a more in-depth

"I told the dean I couldn't go to detention because I have detention-deficit-disorder, and he bought it!"

SOURCE: Copyright © 2003, Aaron Bacall, *The Lighter Side of Teaching*. Thousand Oaks, CA: Corwin Press.

description of the five chronic behavior challenges summarized below and additional disorders as well.

Attention Deficit Disorder

Probably the most frequently diagnosed chronic behavior disorder of students is attention deficit disorder. While the number of American students diagnosed with ADD has increased more than seven times since 1990, nearly 80% of those students taking medication for the disorder are male ("Pay closer attention," 2004). The brain of the ADD child experiences difficulty distinguishing environmental (external) from mental (internal) states, moving from other-directed to self-directed, distinguishing the here and now from the future, and delaying immediate gratification (Jensen, 2000a). In other words, students with attention deficit disorder have a difficult time taking care of their day-to-day responsibilities that require timing and lack of impulsivity. Over 50% of students with ADD appear to have as many as four or more comorbidities. These include stress disorder, depression, oppositional disorder, and drug abuse.

Symptoms of attention deficit disorder include, but are not limited to, the following:

- having a messy desk or area;
- being frequently distracted;
- moving or fidgeting constantly;
- inability to plan sufficiently for future happenings, being unprepared;
- inaccurate sense of the passage of time;
- lacking patience and wanting everything immediately;
- inability to learn from past mistakes and apply to future decisions;
- shouting out answers in class or inability to complete school work.

Conduct Disorder

Often called the predecessor to psychopathic behavior, conduct disorder is probably a teacher's greatest challenge. It is an antisocial, pathological, and extremely disruptive pattern of behavior. Unlike oppositional disorder, conduct disorder is highly tied to violent behavior. It is more prevalent with male than female students. Conduct-disordered students are not the occasionally disruptive learners, but represent a serious and consistent challenge for teachers (Jensen, 2000a).

Symptoms of conduct disorder include, but are not limited to, the following:

- disrupting the classroom with emotional outbursts;
- being consistently disrespectful and cruel to the teacher and classmates;
- using profanity and other forms of verbal abuse;
- committing random acts of violence and destruction against people and animals;

- refusing to follow stated directions;
- blaming others for one's own shortcomings;
- severe lack of social skills;
- perceiving classmates as hostile or threatening.

Learned Helplessness

Learned helplessness, a very serious and chronic condition, occurs when students believe that a certain outcome is inevitable whether or not they respond to the situation. They are often seen as withdrawn and passive because they perceive a lack of ability to control what happens to them. In other words, students with learned helplessness believe that regardless of what they do, they will not be successful, so why try. Learned helplessness is more prevalent in junior and senior high school students than elementary students, students of low socioeconomic status, males, and epileptics, and it can often accompany signs of depression. While serious, learned helplessness is considered a condition, not a disorder, and, therefore, the learned behaviors can be unlearned.

Symptoms of learned helplessness include, but are not limited to, the following:

- making statements like Who cares? So what? Why even try?
- passivity even when events are shocking;
- believing that one has no control over one's environment;
- listlessness and inactivity;
- increased sarcasm;
- decreased amounts of dopamine, serotonin, and epinephrine in the prefrontal cortex of the brain;
- lack of motivation;
- cognitive problems;
- loss of appetite and weight.

Oppositional Disorder

Oppositional disorder, caused by a combination of both genetic and environmental factors, is a chronic disorder of one's personality. Students who exhibit this disorder tend to be aggressive, aggravating, confrontational, and possess a seemingly utter disregard for how other people feel. Unlike students with conduct disorder, these students are not typically violent, although they can be very deceitful, hostile, and aggressive. The number of students with the symptoms of oppositional disorder appears to have increased over the last generation. When paired with attention deficit disorder, oppositional disorder represents the most common psychiatric concern in children. According to Eric Jensen (2000a), as society devalues respect and politeness, the number of students with oppositional disorder is likely to increase.

Symptoms of oppositional disorder include, but are not limited to, the following:

- arguing with adults and peers;
- refusing to follow adult direction, requests, or rules;
- becoming angry and resentful;
- becoming easily annoyed by others;
- cursing or using inappropriate language;
- possessing low self-esteem;
- losing one's temper very easily;
- blaming other people for the mistakes one makes.

Stress Disorder/Depression

Chronic stress is one of the three major sources of the lack of motivation in middle and high school students. The other two are use of marijuana and learned helplessness, which was discussed earlier in this chapter. Repeated incidents of threat and distress are a major problem for about 10% of the student population. These students will experience some of the characteristics of post-traumatic stress disorder and may even experience a marked decrease in the number of cells in the brain stem. When a student's brain is in a high state of stress, it secretes large amounts of cortisol and may respond in one of two ways: either by becoming numb or desensitized to the stress around it, or by becoming hypervigilant or always on alert for the next threatening occurrence.

Symptoms of stress disorder include, but are not limited to, the following:

- bored and listless states;
- losing one's short-term memory;
- lessening of creative thought;
- reduction in social skills;
- lack of ability to concentrate on the task at hand;
- increased rote or automatic behavior;
- decreased energy;
- increased use of drugs such as marijuana and cocaine.

Depression, a chronic, pervasive mood disorder, affects both the mind and body of a student. According to the American Academy of Pediatrics, more than half a million children are taking medication for depression. After puberty, the percentage of female students experiencing some form of depression soars (Jensen, 2000a). Within the last 40 years, suicide rates have tripled. There are several different types of depression: major depression, the most common type; dysthymia, a less serious type typically lasting for several years; bipolar depression, which results in extreme highs and lows in one's personality; and seasonal affective disorder, which follows the rhythm of the seasons of the year and was mentioned in Chapter 4 (Jensen, 2000a).

Symptoms of depression include, but are not limited to, the following:

- lack of interest in most activities;
- persistent sadness, anxiety, or apathy;
- trouble concentrating;
- decreased energy or increased fatigue;
- irritability or uneasiness;
- inability to sleep at night;
- recurring thoughts of death or suicide;
- fluctuation between extreme highs (reckless behavior, impulsivity, great schemes) and extreme lows (withdrawal, apathy, sadness).

The 20 brain-compatible strategies delineated throughout this book are not only necessary for the 90% to 95% of the students whose behavior can be controlled by using the activities in the first 19 chapters, they are also essential for the 5% to 10% whose chronic behavior disorders make your life and the lives of your students challenging, to say the least. When students have the opportunity to visualize themselves being successful and growing in confidence, when they are actively engaged in strategies that require bodily movements such as role-play, drawing, project-based instruction, work-study, or field trips, and when your classroom becomes one in which students see humor, not sarcasm, then, and only then can you come closer to producing students who leave your classroom significantly improved academically, emotionally, and physically.

WHY: THEORETICAL FRAMEWORK

Even the worst-behaving student is acting that way because he or she is receiving something useful from the misbehavior (Kottler, 2002).

Depression and stress increase a student's risk of illness, substance abuse, and suicidal tendencies, especially in adolescents (Sprenger, 2002).

Some students with attention deficit disorder or other neurological problems exhibit behaviors, such as impulsivity, that are not within their control (Kottler, 2002).

In the brain of a student with learned helplessness, cortisol, a stress hormone, may be continuously released and dopamine and serotonin (positive neurotransmitters) depleted (Sprenger, 2002).

Acts of violent behavior, as well as verbal abuse and blatant disrespect, can be very effective in getting a student's needs met and can be a perfect way for the student to exert power (Kottler, 2002).

Established, predictable routines and procedures assist ADHD students in controlling their behaviors, while unpredictability is disconcerting to them (Koenig, 2000).

Students who show signs of conduct disorder may experience diminished levels of the stress hormone cortisol, which causes them to not fear retribution. They could also have reduced activity in the brain's medial prefrontal cortex, which stops aggressive behavior. These two characteristics, in addition to poor parenting skills, appear to predispose students to conduct disorder (Jensen, 2000a).

Until ADHD students can develop internal controls, external controls have to be provided (Koenig, 2000).

Stress reduction techniques such as yoga, art work, singing, positive self-talk, visualization, and movement help students with stress and anxiety disorders (Jensen, 2000a).

Using the *smile and request strategy* with strong-willed or oppositional students will most often result in a positive response (Koenig, 2000, p. 54).

Even students who have completely recovered from mild depression can experience permanent damage to the hippocampus, the part of the brain that is crucial for factual memory (Restak, 2000).

Learned helplessness can be caused by any of the following: (1) neglect, particularly in the early years; (2) a feeling of lack of control during a traumatic experience; (3) parents or teachers who are overprotective and do not allow their children to experience failure; and (4) students who attribute their failures to a defect in their character because they have been taught to believe that they have such a defect (Jensen, 2000a).

In the ADD brain, imaging studies show a lack of activity in the prefrontal cortex, which helps one plan activities and control impulses, and the anterior cingulate, which helps one concentrate and pay attention (Carter, 1998).

Approximately 12% of all students have some sort of brain disorder, such as attention deficit, anxiety disorder, or autism (Koplewicz, 1996).

HOW: CLASSROOM APPLICATION

• Most of the 20 brain-compatible strategies outlined in the Introduction of this book are the same ones recommended for students who exhibit chronic behavior problems. These include increased movement, manipulatives and other hands-on materials, drawing and artwork, music, role-play or drama, project-based instruction, work-study, and games. Perhaps if these strategies were used with all students from the first day of class, many chronic problems would never surface.

• Intervene early with students who display symptoms of these chronic behaviors. Early intervention appears to correlate with a reduction in antisocial behavior as the student ages. For example, with a conduct-disordered student, the most appropriate time to make a change in the behavior is prior to kindergarten, or at least by first grade. By the time this student has become a juvenile, it is much more difficult and often too late (Jensen, 2000a).

- Maintain a positive learning environment in which students can develop a sense of confidence that comes from building on their personal strengths. Celebrate even minimal progress or success that moves the behavior in the intended direction. Catch all students doing something right and praise them for it. Keep progress charts and implement point systems that enable students to earn privileges or affirmations.

- When the ADD brain is threatened, it tends to shut down; therefore, minimize the distress in your classroom and avoid embarrassing the student for the behavior exhibited.

- The following recommendations are made for dealing with the child with an attention deficit disorder:
    o Provide images for students to look at when not paying attention to what the remainder of the class is doing;
    o Involve students in short-term memory activities during the morning hours when they are more focused;
    o Teach using a variety of the multiple intelligences to honor the strengths of all students (see Table I in the Introduction);
    o Determine class rituals and rules and stick to them;
    o Positively reinforce students for appropriate behaviors;
    o Provide opportunities for students to move;
    o Introduce new material in multisensory ways (see Table I in the Introduction) (Sprenger, 2002).

- Remain strong but calm. Any anxiety or overt anger on the part of the teacher who is dealing with these chronic behavior challenges is either a sign of weakness or serves to escalate the confrontation and make the behavior worse. An attitude of calm and strength sends the message that while you are in support of the individual student, you will not tolerate the inappropriate behaviors in your classroom and you cannot be persuaded or threatened to think otherwise.

- Always separate the chronic behavior from the student, realizing that the behavior represents what they are doing and not who they are personally. Examine the situation to ascertain the reason behind the symptoms displayed in class and what you can do to positively affect the disorder, not just temporarily treat the symptoms.

- Do not attempt to deal with any of the aforementioned disorders by yourself. You were probably not trained specifically in this area and must insist on the support of a team of people within and without the school. This team should consist of any of the following persons: the student's parents or guardians, an administrator, a school counselor, social worker, psychiatrist, and the student. Do not perceive this request for support as a sign of weakness. True strength lies in knowing when assistance is warranted so that your classroom can remain the best possible learning environment for every student. For example, my daughter Jennifer, who teaches second grade, is currently dealing with a student whose mother was cocaine addicted when he was born. As a result, he exhibits some characteristics of conduct disorder and learned helplessness. The student exhibits and carries on conversations with several different personalities and is my daughter's biggest challenge this school year. However, with the help of the student's psychiatrist, who he sees several times a week, progress is being made.

- With the support team described above, sit down and make a definitive plan for what will happen with a student when he or she demonstrates certain chronic behaviors. Make sure that each member of the team has input into the plan and that consensus is reached on what the plan will include. In this way, manipulative students cannot play one member of the team against another, and the student will realize that the adults in his or her life are forming a united front. The plan should include the answers to some of the following questions:

  o What strengths does this student have that can be recognized and built upon?
  o What kind of skills need to be developed in this student, and how can we specifically go about developing those skills?
  o What is the time frame for the development of the necessary skills?
  o Where should this student sit in the room?
  o Which of the classroom rules will be enforced and which overlooked in the case of this student?
  o What will be the plan if this student disrupts class, bothers another student, or refuses to do the assigned work?
  o What will be the plan if this student becomes violent or throws a temper tantrum?
  o When is the best time for the support team to meet, and how often? (Jensen, 2000a)

- Play calming music as students enter your classroom, during transition times, or when students are engaged in creative tasks. Classical, jazz, Celtic, Native American, or New Age music enables the brain and body to relax and places it in more of a state conducive for learning. Set up a listening station or use earphones when you only desire that certain students avail themselves of specific music. See Chapter 5 for additional information on the use of music in the classroom.

- Make your classroom highly predictable by establishing your routines and procedures from the first day of school and practicing them until they become habitual. Open and close class the same way daily. Make transitions predictable. Your ADD student, especially, will thank you. When there does need to be a change in the routine, make students aware of the change prior to its implementation.

- Break the content and the accompanying activities into chunks so that even students with short attention spans remain focused. Tell students how much time they have for each learning segment, and provide warnings prior to the time to change to the next activity.

- Students who experience learned helplessness feel a lack of control over what they are experiencing. A sense of control can be encouraged through the following: providing students with choices and discussing the consequences of those choices, supplying students with an overview of the day's activities in advance, allowing them time to journal and discuss with others, and incorporating movement into the lesson (Sprenger, 2002).

- With oppositional, conduct disordered, or other strong-willed students, smile and request a change in behavior. Then move away from the student's space. For example, if John is talking out of turn, simply say, "John, would you consider not talking when I am talking?" and then move away from the student's desk.

- Work-study is one of the most prevalent brain-compatible strategies used in alternative schools throughout the country. These schools are populated by middle and high school students who, for whatever reason, have been suspended or expelled from traditional school. Many of these students are there because they have demonstrated symptoms of the chronic behavior challenges that we have been discussing. Work-study, which includes apprenticeships, internships, and other forms of on-the-job training, not only provides students with active engagement but supplies them with the life purposes that are so sorely lacking. When students in alternative schools can spend time reading once or twice a week to the senior citizens in a retirement home; design original pieces of artwork to be sold to the community; plant flowers to beautify the school campus; or plan, cook, and serve delicious meals to the culinary delight of all who partake, positive brain chemicals are produced and negative self-perceptions are replaced with confidence. A confident student seldom disrupts. In my house hangs a beautiful painting that represents the creative efforts of a student in McArthur South Alternative School in Miami, Florida where I taught for several days. Every time I look at that painting, I have hope.

- Consult Chapter 15, Accentuate the Positive, and Chapter 18, Deemphasize the Negative, for additional classroom activities that may work with your most challenging students as well as all others in your room.

REFLECTION

> ### What is my specific plan for dealing with the chronic behavior disorders in my classroom?

Attention Deficit Disorder

_____

_____

_____

Conduct Disorder

_____

_____

_____

Learned Helplessness

_____

_____

_____

Oppositional Disorder

_____

_____

_____

Stress Disorder/Depression

_____

_____

_____

Other Chronic Disorder

_____

_____

_____

20

Solicit Parental Support

WHAT: PARENTS ON YOUR SIDE

Just because this is the last chapter in the book does not mean it is any less important than the 19 chapters that precede it. In fact, parents are their children's first and best teachers. Just as I don't believe that any teacher gets up in the morning with the intention of not doing a good job at teaching, I also don't feel that any parent gets up in the morning determined to be the worst possible parent he or she can be. In most cases, I surmise that parents are doing the best they can based on the knowledge, skills, experiences, and circumstances in which they find themselves.

While the job of a parent is so important, it also does not come with a manual. There are very few courses, if any, to prepare parents for the mammoth job that they are about to undertake. If there were an ad placed for the job of a parent, if might read as follows:

WANTED: PARENT

Must have the skills of a doctor, lawyer, nurse, teacher, counselor, and referee
Must maintain a sense of humor even in the most stressful times
Must be able to operate a taxi service to and from all important events
No pay, lots of overtime
In fact, on call 24 hours a day
No sick days allowed
Lifetime commitment

If this ad truly did appear in your local paper, would you hurry to apply? Who would? As an educator and a parent of three, I know that both jobs are arduous assignments. Many teachers and administrators view today's parents with emotions that range from cautious optimism to downright disdain. There is a reason for the variations in feelings toward parent support and involvement. According to McEwan (2002), many parents of students today tend to be more personally informed and actively engaged in education, but also less respectful of authority and more cynical, distrustful, stressed, angry, and worried than ever before. On the other hand, some parents appear not to care at all.

McEwan (2002) further states that parents are displaying increased hostility for some of the following reasons: a failure of the school to communicate, educators' unwillingness to keep commitments, educators becoming defensive when practices are called into question or being unable to apologize when an apology is warranted, or educators being unwilling to give parents credit for truly understanding their children and having insight into school challenges.

In Chapter 15 we discussed the concept of the emotional bank account. Let's apply that to the teacher-parent connection. Let's suppose that the first contact a parent has with you at the beginning of the school year is negative. For example, school has just started and you call to complain because Johnny is out of his seat when he's not supposed to be. Well, you are on the deficit side of Johnny's parents' bank account and the year has just begun. If these negative contacts (or withdrawals) continue, then soon you are overdrawn with this parent and may even bankrupt the relationship. When parents stop taking your calls and refuse to attend

"Angry parents on lines 1, 2, 3, 4, and 5."

parent-teacher conferences, you might want to consider that you are involved in a bankrupt relationship.

It is so vitally important that the initial contact with a student's parent be positive. This contact can determine whether you establish a year-long supportive or adversarial relationship with the most important people in your students' lives. This positive phone call, or deposit, helps to ensure that if it becomes necessary for you to make a withdrawal (a contact for a negative reason), there will be a balance in the account.

Whether dealing with two-parent families, single-parent families, teen parent families, step-parent families, or no-parent families, students excel when their teacher and parent or caregiver enjoy a positive relationship (Rudney, 2005). Just as in proactive classroom management, proactive, positive relationships with parents can result in fewer reactive interactions and angry confrontations.

WHY: THEORETICAL FRAMEWORK

When parents and teachers are partners in educating students, a more unified home-school effort exists and they are less likely to lay blame on one another when anything is amiss (Orange, 2005).

Often parents of children living in poverty will side with their child against the teacher in an effort to survive (Rudney, 2005).

Teachers often blame parents for the problems their students encounter in school (Kottler, 2002).

Every school will promote partnerships that will increase parental involvement and participation in promoting social, emotional, and academic growth of children (U. S. Department of Education, 2002, p. 1).

Parents who give teachers the most difficulty can be described as follows:

- the parent who expects every teacher to cater to their individual needs;
- the parent who is full of hostility and anger;
- the parent who will never believe that his or her child can ever be responsible for any misbehavior;
- the parent who manipulates the situation and works from a secret agenda;
- the parent who is out of control; and
- the parent who has no earthly idea how to be a parent or to deal with the child's inappropriate behavior (Kottler, 2002).

Parents want teachers who exhibit the personal traits of character, who can teach traits that obtain results, and who demonstrate the intellect of knowledge and awareness (McEwan, 2002).

For every child with a brain disorder of some kind, there is a parent and or teacher who blames himself or herself for being unable to effectively discipline that child (Kottler, 2002).

The majority of students report that their parents do know how well they are doing in school (Metropolitan Life, 2002).

The job of every teacher is to win the support and assistance of every parent (Kottler, 2002).

When there is excellent parent-teacher communication, positive relationships are built before problems occur (Whitaker & Fiore, 2001).

When parents are involved in their child's education, the child's opportunity to be successful in the classroom increases (Koenig, 2000).

Fathers have often felt ignored by schools who expect that the mothers in the family will follow through on the decisions made (Galinsky, 2001).

Parents determine how competent a teacher is according to the following criteria:

- ability to manage the students;
- attempts to work cooperatively with parents;
- ability to be organized; and
- ability to balance negative and positive feedback regarding their child (Koenig, 2000).

When a survey was conducted of more than 1,000 teachers, 71% of them agreed that a deficit in parent supervision at home was the major factor in increased school violence (Metropolitan Life Insurance Company, 1993).

HOW: CLASSROOM APPLICATION

• Administrators should be encouraged to involve parents, business leaders, community members, and other stakeholders in strategic planning activities. Create surveys to solicit input on crucial school-related issues and involve volunteers on teams that are trained to develop action plans to accomplish school goals and objectives. Parents will not object to plans they personally helped to develop.

• Administrators should determine who the *key communicators* are in the community. These are the *movers and shakers* who carry a great deal of influence and should be invited to the school and constantly kept abreast of the specific school goals and progress toward those goals.

• Prior to the beginning of the school year, if possible, make a personal contact with every prospective parent. Call, write, or e-mail each parent expressing your anticipation at having their child in your classroom for the year and informing them of your positive expectations for their child's success. If the initial contact is positive (a deposit), subsequent contacts will be more well-received. This is much more easily accomplished at the elementary level. However, teachers at the middle and high school level could make the initial contact in writing.

• Secure the e-mail address of every parent willing to give it to you. Set up a file and a consistent system for informing parents of general information regarding your classroom, such as rituals and procedures, current academic objectives, upcoming field trips, assemblies, and so on.

• Create a Web page of your own or become a part of your school's Web site. Post important class happenings and communicate with parents as they access your site. Weekly homework assignments and dates for weekly, mid-term, and final exams should be posted.

• Share your specific classroom management plan in writing with all of your students' parents. Have each student take a copy of the plan home and have parents or guardians sign, stating that they have read the plan and discussed it with the student. For non-English-speaking parents, have the plan translated into the predominant language(s) spoken by the students in your room.

• Take time to share the good news from your classroom in a newsletter or just a brief e-mail. Let parents know when students have great weeks following your rituals and procedures, when the average percentage of students passing your tests improves, or when an individual student excels. Shout the good news from the rooftops!

• Invite your students' parents or guardians to serve as volunteers in your classroom whenever possible. Once they see firsthand the awesome responsibility that you have as their child's teacher, they may be more supportive of what you are trying to accomplish. If you are not comfortable with them volunteering for you, recommend that they volunteer in another capacity in the school.

• Invite your students' parents or guardians to accompany the class on field trips and other class excursions. For example, my daughter Jennifer teaches second grade. Each year, I accompany her and her class to the holiday performance of the Atlanta Ballet's *Nutcracker*. Prior to the performance, the students and their parents dine with us at The Spaghetti Factory, a local restaurant. Not only does the excursion teach the students proper skills for formal dining, but they experience the artistry of a beautiful ballet. There is also a side benefit that I don't believe my daughter even expected—the gratitude, support, and commitment of those parents who accompany us. That support lasts for the remainder of the school year and beyond. My daughter is one of the most loved teachers in her school by the parents of her students. She's also a wonderful teacher (if I do say so, myself)!

- When conducting a parent-teacher conference, be sure you adhere to the following guidelines:
    - Begin and end the conference on time;
    - Greet the parents cordially and tell them how happy you are to have their child in your class and that you are looking forward to working together;
    - Share the purpose and agenda of the conference and stick to it;
    - Share some positive news regarding the student's attributes or abilities;
    - State your concern and ask the parents what they think should be done about it;
    - Attempt to reach consensus as to next steps;
    - End with courtesy and a positive statement about future meetings.

REFLECTION

> **What are some specific steps I can take to establish positive relationships with my students' parents/guardians?**

1. _____

_____

2. _____

_____

3. _____

_____

4. _____

_____

5. _____

_____

6. _____

_____

7. _____

_____

8. _____

_____

9. _____

_____

10. _____

_____

Bibliography

Amabile, T. (1989). *Growing up creative.* New York: Crown.

Bartlett, D. (1996). Physiological responses to music and sound stimuli. In D. Hodges (Ed.), *Handbook of music psychology* (pp. 343–385). San Antonio, TX: IMR Press.

Beamon, G. W. (2001). *Teaching with adolescent learning in mind.* Arlington Heights, IL: Skylight Professional Development.

Belvel, P. S., & Jordan, M. M. (2003). *Rethinking classroom management: Strategies for prevention, intervention, and problem solving.* Thousand Oaks, CA: Corwin Press.

Bloom's Taxonomy. (n. d.). Retrieved January 16, 2000, from www.teachers.ash.org .au/researchskills/dalton.htm

Boeree, C. G. (1998). *Abraham Maslow, 1908–1970.* Retrieved December 15, 2005, from www.ship.edu/~cgboeree/maslow.html

Boyatzis, C. J., & Varghese, R. (1994, March). Children's emotional associations with colors. *Journal of Genetic Psychology, 155*(1), 77–85.

Burden, P. R. (2000). *Powerful classroom management strategies: Motivating students to learn.* Thousand Oaks, CA: Corwin Press.

Burgess, R. (2000). *Laughing lessons: 149 2/3 ways to make teaching and learning fun.* Minneapolis, MN: Free Spirit.

Burke, K. (1992). *What to do with the kid who: Developing cooperation, self-discipline, and responsibility in the classroom.* Thousand Oaks, CA: Corwin Press.

Burns, M. (2003). The battle for civilized behavior. *Phi Delta Kappan, 84*(7), 546–550.

Cacioppo, J. T., Gardner, W. L., & Berntson, G. G. (1999). The affect system has parallel and integrative processing components. Form follows function. *Journal of Personality and Social Psychology, 76,* 839–855.

Canter, L., & Canter, M. (1993). *Suceeding with difficult students.* Santa Monica, CA: Canter & Associates.

Carney, R. N., & Levin, J. R. (2000). Mnemonic instruction, with a focus on transfer. *Journal of Educational Psychology, 92*(4), 783–790.

Carter, R. (1998). *Mapping the mind.* Los Angeles: University of California Press.

Cawelti, G. (Ed.). (1995). *Handbook of research on improving student achievement.* Arlington, VA: Educational Research Service.

Chapman, C., & King, R. (2003). *Differentiated instructional strategies for reading in the content areas.* Thousand Oaks, CA: Corwin Press.

College Board. (2000). *The College Board: Preparing, inspiring, and connecting.* Retrieved December 15, 2005, from www.collegeboard.org/prof

Covino, J. K. (2002). Mind matters. *District Administrator, 38*(2), 25–27.

Crawford, G. B. (2004). *Managing the adolescent classroom: Lessons from outstanding teachers.* Thousand Oaks, CA: Corwin Press.

Csikszentmihalyi, M., & Csikszentmihalyi, I. (1990). *The psychology of optimal experience.* New York: Harper & Row.

Dale, E. (1969). *Audio-visual methods in teaching* (3rd ed.). New York: Holt, Reinhart & Winston.

Davis, B. M. (2006). *How to teach students who don't look like you: Culturally relevant teaching strategies.* Thousand Oaks, CA: Corwin Press.

Deci, E. L., Koestner, R., & Ryan, R. M. (1999). *A meta-analytic review of experiments examining the effects of extrinsic rewards on intrinsic motivation.* Retrieved December 15, 2005, from www.psych.rochester.edu/SDT/cont_reward.html

Dember, W., & Parasuraman, R. (1993). Remarks before the American Association for the Advancement of Science. In P. J. Howard (Ed.), *The owner's manual for the brain: Everyday applications from mind-brain research,* Austin, TX: Leornian Press.

Dennison, G. E. (1990). *The big vision book.* Ventura, CA: Edu-Kinesthetics.

Dhong, H. J., Chung, S. K., & Doty, R. L. (1999, April). Estrogen protects against 3-methylindole-induced olfactory loss. *Brain Research, 824*(2), 312–315.

Dhyan, S. (1995, September). The transforming force of laughter with the focus on the laughing meditation. *Patient Education and Counseling, 26*(1–3), 367–371.

DiGiulio, R. (2000). *Positive classroom management* (2nd ed.). Thousand Oaks, CA: Corwin Press.

Divinyi, J. (2003). *Discipline that works: 5 simple steps.* Peachtree City, GA: The Wellness Connection.

Dougherty, R. (1997). Grade/study performance contracts, enhanced communication, cooperative learning, and student performance in undergraduate organic chemistry. *Journal of Chemical Education, 74*(6), 722–726.

Engen, T. (1991). *Odor sensation and memory.* New York: Praeger.

Erlauer, L. (2003). *The brain-compatible classroom: Using what we know about learning to improve teaching.* Alexandria, VA: Association for Supervision and Curriculum Development.

Feigelson, S. (1998). *Energize your meetings with laughter.* Alexandria, VA: Association for Supervision and Curriculum Development.

Feinstein, S. (2004). *Secrets of the teenage brain: Research-based strategies for reaching and teaching today's adolescents.* Thousand Oaks, CA: Corwin Press.

Galinsky, E. (2001, April). What children want from parents. *Educational Leadership, 58*(7), 24–28.

Gardner, H. (1983). *Frames of mind: The theory of multiple intelligences.* New York: Basic Books.

Glasser, W. (1999). *Choice theory.* New York: Perennial.

Gregory, G., & Chapman, C. (2002). *Differentiated instructional strategies. One size doesn't fit all.* Thousand Oaks, CA: Corwin Press.

Guskey, T. R. (2001, Summer). The backward approach. *Journal of Staff Development, 22*(3), 60.

Hannaford, C. (1995). *Smart moves: Why learning is not all in your head.* Arlington, VA: Great Oceans.

Harmon, D. B. (1951). *The coordinated classroom* (Research paper). Grand Rapids, MI: The American Seating Company.

Haycock, K. (2001). Closing the achievement gap. *Educational Leadership, 58*(6), 6–11.

Heschong, L. (1999). *Daylighting in schools: An investigation into the relationship between daylighting and human performance.* A study performed on behalf of the California Board for Energy Efficiency for the Third Party Program administered by Pacific Gas & Electric, as part of the PG & E contract 460–000.

Jensen, E. (1994). *The learning brain.* San Diego, CA: Turning Point.

Jensen, E. (1995). *Brain-based learning and teaching.* Thousand Oaks, CA: Corwin Press.

Jensen, E. (1996). *Completing the puzzle: The brain-based approach.* Thousand Oaks, CA: Corwin Press.

Jensen, E. (1997). *Completing the puzzle. The brain-compatible approach to learning.* Thousand Oaks, CA: Corwin Press.

Jensen, E. (1998). *Sizzle and substance. Presenting with the brain in mind.* Thousand Oaks, CA: Corwin Press.

Jensen, E. (2000a). *Different learners, different brains: How to reach the hard to teach.* Thousand Oaks, CA: Corwin Press.

Jensen, E. (2000b). Moving with the brain in mind. *Educational Leadership, 58*(3), 34–37.

Jensen, E. (2001). *Arts with the brain in mind.* Alexandria, VA: Association for Supervision and Curriculum Development.

Jensen, E. (2003). *Tools for engagement: Managing emotional states for learner success.* Thousand Oaks, CA: Corwin Press.

Jensen, E., & Dabney, M. (2000). *Learning smarter: The new science of teaching.* Thousand Oaks, CA: Corwin Press.

Johnson, R. S. (2002). *Using data to close the achievement gap: How to measure equity in our schools.* Thousand Oaks, CA: Corwin Press.

Jones, F. (2000). *Tools for teaching.* Santa Cruz, CA: Jones & Associates.

Kerman, S. (1979). Teacher expectation and student achievement. *Phi Delta Kappan, 60,* 716–718.

Koenig, L. (2000). *Smart discipline for the classroom: Respect and cooperation restored* (3rd ed.). Thousand Oaks, CA: Corwin Press.

Kohn, A. (1993). *Punished by rewards.* New York: Houghton Mifflin.

Koplewicz, H. S. (1996). *It's nobody's fault: New hope for difficult children.* New York: Times Books.

Kottler, J. A. (2002). *Students who drive you crazy: Succeeding with resistant, unmotivated, and otherwise difficult young people.* Thousand Oaks, CA: Corwin Press.

Kounin, J. S. (1970). *Discipline and group management in classrooms.* New York: Holt, Rinehart & Winston.

Krepel, W. J., & Duvall, C. R. (1981). *Field trips: A guide for planning and conducting educational experiences.* Washington, DC: National Education Association.

Krimsky, J. S. (1982). *A comparative analysis of the effects of matching and mismatching fourth grade students with their learning style preferences for the environmental element of light and their subsequent reading speed and accuracy scores.* Unpublished doctoral dissertation, Saint John's University, MN.

Lazear, E. P. (2000). Performance pay and productivity. *American Economic Review, 90*(51), 1346–1361.

Levine, J., Baukol, P., & Pavlidis, I. (1999). The energy expended in chewing gum. *New England Journal of Medicine, 341,* 2100.

Lewis, T., Amini, B., & Lannon, R. (2000). *A general theory of love.* New York: Random House.

Los Angeles County Office of Education. (1972). *Teacher expectations and student achievement (TESA).* Los Angeles: Author.

MacLaughlin, J. A., Anderson, R. R., & Holic, M. F. (1982, May). Spectral character of sunlight modulates photosynthesis of previtamin D3 and its photo-isomers in human skin. *Science, 216*(4549), 1001–1003.

Markowitz, K., & Jensen, E. (1999). *The great memory book.* Thousand Oaks, CA: Corwin Press.

Marzano, R. (2004). *Building background knowledge for academic achievement.* Alexandria, VA: Association for Supervisors and Curriculum Developers.

Marzano, R. J., Pickering, D. J., & Pollok, J. E. (2001). *Classroom instruction that works: Research-based strategies for increasing student achievement.* Alexandria, VA: Association for Supervision and Curriculum Development.

McEwan, E. K. (2002). *10 traits of highly effective teachers: How to hire, coach, and mentor successful teachers.* Thousand Oaks, CA: Corwin Press.

McEwan, E. K., & Damer, M. (2000). *Managing unmanageable students.* Thousand Oaks, CA: Corwin Press.

Meany, M. J., Sapolsky, R. M., & McEwen, B. S. (1985, February). The development of the glucocorticoid receptor system in the rat limbic brain II. An autoradiographic study. *Developmental Brain Research, 350*(1–2), 165–168.

Metropolitan Life Insurance Company. (1993). *The Metropolitan Life survey of the American teacher, 1993: Violence in America's public schools.* New York: Author.

Metropolitan Life. (2002). *The Metlife survey of the American teacher, 2002: Student life—School, home, and community.* Retrieved December 26, 2005, from www.metlife.com/Applications/Corporate/WPS/CDA/PageGenerator/0,1 674,P2817,00.html

Michalon, M., Eskes, G., & Mate-Kole, C. (1997, January). Effects of light therapy on neuropsychological function and mood in seasonal affective disorder. *Journal of Psychiatry & Neuroscience, 22*(1), 19–28.

Nargundkar, V. (2001). *Seven keys to unlock your brain power.* Retrieved December 15, 2005, from www.boloji.com/ayurveda/av012.htm

Nieto, S. (1999). *Affirming diversity: The sociopolitical context of multicultural education* (3rd ed.). Reading, MA: Addison-Wesley.

O'Connor, P. D., Sofo, F., Kendall, L., & Olsen, G. (1988). Reading disabilities and the effects of colored filters. *Journal of Reading.* Retrieved December 15, 2005, from www.DyslexiaCure.com

Orange, C. (2005). *Smart strategies for avoiding classroom mistakes.* Thousand Oaks, CA: Corwin Press.

Padgett, D. A., Sheridan, J. F., Dorne, J., Berntson, G. G., Candelora, J., & Glaser, R. (1998, June 9). Social stress and the reactivation of latent herpes simplex virus type I. *Proceedings of the National Academy of Sciences of the United States of America, 95*(12), 7231–7235.

Pauli, P., Bourne, L. E., Diekmann, H., & Birbaumer, N. (1999). Cross-modality priming between odor-congruent words. *American Journal of Psychology, 112*(2), 175.

Pay closer attention: Boys are struggling academically. (2004, December 2). *USA Today,* p. 12A.

Payne, R. K. (2001). *A framework for understanding poverty* (Rev. ed.). Highlands, TX: Aha! Process.

Pert, C. (1997). *Molecules of emotion: Why you feel the way you feel.* New York: Scribner.

Read, M., Sugawara, A., & Brandt, J. (1999, May). Impact of space and color in the physical environment on preschool children's cooperative behavior. *Environment and Behavior, 31*(3), 413–414.

Report of the National Reading Panel. (2000). *Teaching children to read.* Jessup, MD: National Institute for Literacy at EDPubs.

Restak, R. (2000). *Mysteries of the mind.* Washington, DC: National Georgraphic.

Rickelman, R. J., & Henk, W. A. (1990). Colored overlays and tinted lens filters. *The Reading Teacher.* Retrieved December 15, 2005, from www.DyslexiaCure. com

Rosenthal, R., & Jacobson, L. (1992). *Pygmalion in the classroom: Teacher expectation and pupils' intellectual development.* New York: Irvington.

Rudney, G. L. (2005). *Every teacher's guide to working with parents.* Thousand Oaks, CA: Corwin Press.

Rutherford, P. (2002). *Why didn't I learn this in college? Teaching and learning in the 21st century.* Alexandria, VA: Just Ask Publications.

Schiller, P. (2001). *Brain research and its implications for early childhood programs.* Retrieved December 15, 2005, from http://www.southernearlychildhood .org/position_brain.html

Schnaubelt, K. (1999). *Advanced aromatherapy: Healing with essential oils.* Berkeley, CA: Frog.

Shaie, K. W., & Heiss, R. (1964). *Color and personality.* Bern, Switzerland: Hans Huber.

Shammin, P., & Stuss, D. T. (1999, April). Humour appreciation: A role of the right frontal lobe. *Brain, 123*(4), 657–666.

Silver, H., Strong, R., & Perini, M. (2000). *So each may learn: Integrating learning styles and multiple intelligences.* Alexandria, VA: Association for Supervision and Curriculum Development.

Sinclair, R. C., Soldat, A., & Mark, M. M. (1998). Affective cues and processing strategy: Color-coded examination forms influence performance. *Teaching of Psychology, 25*(2), 130–132.

Smith, R. (2004). *Conscious classroom management: Unlocking the secrets of great teaching.* San Rafael, CA: Conscious Teaching Publications.

Society for Developmental Education. (1995). *Pyramid of learning.* Peterborough, NH: Author.

Sousa, D. (2001). *How the brain learns* (2nd ed.). Thousand Oaks, CA: Corwin Press.

Sprenger, M. (1999). *Learning and memory. The brain in action.* Alexandria, VA: Association for Supervision and Curriculum Development.

Sprenger, M. (2002). *Becoming a wiz at brain-based teaching: How to make every year a best year.* Thousand Oaks, CA: Corwin Press.

Sprenger, M. (2005). *How to teach so students remember.* Alexandria, VA: Association for Supervision and Curriculum Development.

Sternberg, R. J., & Grigorenko, E. L. (2000). *Teaching for successful intelligence: To increase student learning and achievement.* Thousand Oaks, CA: Corwin Press.

Sullivan, T. E., Schefft, B. K., Warm, J. S., & Dember, W. N. (1998, April). Effects of olfactory stimulation on the vigilance performance of individuals with brain injury. *Journal of Clinical and Experimental Neuropsychology, 20*(2), 227–236.

Sylwester, R. (1997). The neurobiology of self-esteem and aggression. *Educational Leadership, 54,* 75–79.

Tate, M. L. (2003). *Worksheets don't grow dendrites: 20 instructional strategies that engage the brain.* Thousand Oaks, CA: Corwin Press.

Tate, M. (2004). *"Sit and get" won't grow dendrites: 20 professional learning strategies that engage the adult brain.* Thousand Oaks, CA: Corwin Press.

Tate, M. (2005). *Reading and language arts worksheets don't grow dendrites: 20 literacy strategies that engage the brain.* Thousand Oaks, CA: Corwin Press.

Thayer, R. (1996). *The origin of everyday moods* (pp. 128–132). New York: Oxford University Press.

Thiers, N. (Ed.). (1995). *Successful strategies: Building a school-to-careers system.* Alexandria, VA: American Vocational Association.

Tileston, D. W. (2004). *What every teacher should know about classroom management and discipline.* Thousand Oaks, CA: Corwin Press.

U. S. Department of Education. (1986). *What works: Research about teaching and learning.* Washington, DC: U. S. Government Printing Office.

U. S. Department of Education. (2002, January 8). *Online newsletter.* Retrieved December 15, 2005, from www.ed.gov/nclb/landing.jhtml

U. S. Secretary's Commission on Achieving Necessary Skills. (1991). *What work requires of schools: A SCANS report for America 2000.* Washington, DC: U.S. Department of Labor.

van Toller, S. (1988). Odors and the brain. In S. van Toller & G. Dodd (Eds.), *Perfumery: The psychology and biology of fragrance* (pp. 121–146). London: Chapman & Hall.

Wallace, D. S., West, S. W., Ware, D. F., & Dansereau, D. (1998, Fall). The effect of knowledge maps that incorporate gestalt principles on learning. *Journal of Experimental Education, 67*(1), 5–16.

Webb, D., & Webb, T. (1990). *Accelerated learning with music.* Norcross, GA: Accelerated Learning Systems.

Whitaker, T., & Fiore, D. J. (2001). *Dealing with difficult parents and with parents in difficult situations.* Larchmont, NY: Eye on Education.

Wolfe, P. (2001). *Brain matters: Translating research into classroom practice.* Alexandria, VA: Association for Supervision and Curriculum Development.

Wong, H. K., & Wong, R. T. (1998). *The first days of school: How to be an effective teacher.* Mountain View, CA: Harry K. Wong.

Index

Punishment
  ineffectiveness of, 103–104
  writing as form of, 106

Questions
  Bloom's taxonomy level for, 11
  incorrect answers to, 12
  from students to peers, 74

Read, M., 32, 132
Real-life projects, 58, 60
Recognition, 85
Red, 31–33
Reinforcers, 87–88
Relevance of learning
  benefits of, 54
  description of, 57–58
  instructional strategies for promoting,
    58–59
Restak, R., 115, 132
Reteaching, 72–73
Rewards
  alternatives to, 85, 87
  drawbacks of, 85–86
  uses of, 84, 87
Rickelman, R. J., 32, 132
Rituals
  development of, 4
  students' participation in creating, 66
  teaching of, 63–67, 86, 105
Role-play
  examples of, 79
  uses of, xvi
Rosemary, 36
Rosenthal, R., 7, 132
Rudney, G. L., 123, 132
Rutherford, P., 132
Ryan, R. M., 84, 130

Sapolsky, R. M., 73, 132
Sarcasm, 45–46
Schefft, B. K., 36, 133
Schiller, P., 36, 132
Schnaubelt, K., 132
School-to-career initiatives, 59
Scotopic sensitivity, 32
Seasonal affective disorder, 22, 113
Seating arrangements
  alternative methods, xiii, 42
  description of, 40–43
  flexible, 43
Self-esteem, 9
Self-systems, 53, 59
Serotonin, 78
Shaie, K. W., 32, 133

Shammin, P., 46, 133
Sheridan, J. F., 73, 132
Signaling, 98
Silver, H., 133
Sinclair, R. C., 32, 133
Smith, R., 2, 17, 41, 85, 103, 133
Socialization, 71
Social reinforcers, 88
Sofo, F., 32, 132
Soldat, A., 32, 133
Sousa, D., 3, 26, 28, 46, 78, 85, 92, 133
Sprenger, M., 25, 39, 52, 59,
    65, 114, 118, 133
Standing in classroom, 40, 43
Sternberg, R. J., xv, 9, 133
Stress, 73, 86
Stress disorder, 113–115
Stretch break, 80
Strong, R., 133
Student(s)
  acting out by, 17
  age of, 73
  aggressive behavior by, 104
  angry, 104–105
  asking questions, 11
  attention seeking by, 15–18
  behavioral expectations for, 64
  calling on, 11
  calming of, 26–28
  complimenting of, 18
  control by, 16–17, 19
  embarrassment fears of, 11–12
  feelings of success by, 3
  getting to know, 18, 86
  goal setting by, 59
  interest of, 3
  peer questioning by, 74
  personal interest in, 18, 86
  praising of, 85, 87, 92
  raising of voice by, 99
  reteaching by, 72–73
  rituals created by, 66
  self-systems of, 53, 59
  talking in classroom by, 71–74
Stuss, D. T., 46, 133
Success
  celebration for, 4, 87
  intelligence and, 9
  misbehavior and, 3
Sugawara, A., 32, 132
Sullivan, T. E., 36, 133
Sylwester, R., 92, 133

Tangible reinforcers, 87–88
Tarts, 37

**CORWIN
PRESS**

The Corwin Press logo—a raven striding across an open book—represents the union of courage and learning. Corwin Press is committed to improving education for all learners by publishing books and other professional development resources for those serving the field of PreK–12 education. By providing practical, hands-on materials, Corwin Press continues to carry out the promise of its motto: **"Helping Educators Do Their Work Better."**